First published in 2020 in the United Kingdom, by Simon D. Gary.
Edited and typeset by MJV Literary Author Services.

ISBN:
e-Book: 978-1-9160525-2-9
Paperback: 978-1-9160525-3-6

www.simondgary.com

Kaizen Your Life

Simon D. Gary

TABLE OF CONTENTS

INTRODUCTION

For decades, the biggest businesses in the world have deployed continuous improvement techniques to cement their place at the top of the tree. This dominance has been no accident. In the case of Toyota, this preeminence has come via the unrelenting application of the Toyota Production System, which itself has been much admired and copied across the globe. This system laid the foundation of Kaizen, the Japanese art of Continuous Improvement.

If this philosophy can drive companies to great success, then can it be adapted to bring some measure of success to our own individual lives? This book seeks to explore that.

Uniquely, and unlike any other publication of this nature, I will be applying the ideas that I am describing alongside you. I am not writing this from the point of view of a successful person; I have the same issues and demons as you do. My progress will be your progress. I am not writing this from the comfortable distance of wealth and achievement. We will truly be working together.

And, so the journey begins.

1

SO, WHY CHANGE?

Change is challenging to sell in a business environment, and it is no different when we take on this task as individuals.

Kotter's Change Model describes the first step on the path as: *"Create the urgency for change".* In other words, you should be thinking: *Wow, it is time that I did something about this?* to such a level of desire that the pain of staying where you are outweighs the pain of change.

Allow me to let you into a secret; this is how I know this fact is true: I am a problem gambler. Although I have not placed a bet in what must be ten years, I would still label myself as such. Like the alcoholic, if I return to this habit, I might be fine for a few weeks - or even a few months - but, eventually, there is an overriding chance (if you'll pardon the expression) that I will soon be back gambling, with as much, or even more, destructive zeal as I was previously; if I went deep last time, I would go even deeper the next! I dare say that these are experiences which I will draw on a lot, throughout this piece. It now feels like the time is right to draw something positive from them.

The point which I am working towards is this: in order to begin to see – and, I mean to *really* see - that I needed to stop gambling, I had to get to a point from where there was no place else to go. Family and friends may have told me continually that I needed to stop, but I would not have heard them; I knew better. That big, life-transforming win, or lucky streak, was always just around the corner. I'd had my share of bad luck, so wasn't it time that I got some good luck?

Well, the short answer to this is no. The Universe does not work that way. There isn't some cosmological balance sheet, which tots up all of your misfortunes and decides that you have had enough. The only thing which will inspire real, lasting change in your life is you.

So, what is it that you want to achieve? What is the nature of the pain you are experiencing? Do you *want* to change? Do you want it with every atom of your being? At the moment, you might not be in a place from which you feel that you can even begin working toward something positive - some sea change, which will astound family and friends. That's okay. We will talk more about that later, when we address goals and objective setting.

But, for now, let's begin to build some momentum. Let

us apply the logic of starting small, with something of which we are all capable. This is a book about action, and our first action must start now.

2

WORKPLACE ORGANIZATION

"Workplace Organization", or *"5S"*, as it is often called, is the foundation upon which all lean techniques are constructed.

If you were building a house, you would make sure that the foundations were strong; you cannot build on sand. The same is true of personal improvement. When we start by putting the basics in place, we can gather tremendous momentum and send a positive message to the Universe, regarding our intentions. *5S* is a great place to begin.

Like many business improvement techniques, *5S* has its origins in Japan. The *5S* began life as the following:

SEIRI – SEITON – SEISO – SEIKETSU - SHITSUKE.

They have been translated many times, and different variants have emerged. Here are the five which we will be using in the main:

SORT – SET – SHINE - STANDARDIZE – SUSTAIN.

So, let's take a look at each of these in turn.

SORT

The first of the *5S* is a very liberating one.

Now, I have to admit that as a single man, working long hours, I have long lived in a home which more closely resembles a rubbish tip. How did this make me feel? It made me feel depressed. Moreover, the messier it got, the harder it became to find a starting point; the house grew untidier, and I became more depressed and unmotivated.

If I had seen this same situation in the workplace, I would have undoubtedly deployed *5S*. Therefore, that is what I had to do at home, too.

So, what is the objective of *SORT*? We can answer that question by asking another: essentially, it is about handling everything in your house and asking yourself: "Do I need this item or not?" It is about removing clutter and, especially in the home, about letting go of things. In this step, you need to reduce everything to a binary output: *need* or *no need*.

In the workplace, unrequired items are sent to a quarantine area, just in case it turns out that they are needed later, or somebody else could use them. But, in the case of your personal items, you may choose not to follow this step. See, the problem with items stored in workplace quarantine areas is that they have a tendency to "float" back into the factory or office space. When applying personal *SORT*, you'll have to be a lot more brutal.

It was only when I started applying *SORT* for myself, personally, that I realized how much difficulty I experienced in actually throwing things away. There were items I had not so much as looked at in months, or even years, yet still I found the idea of throwing them away appalling.

So, handle every item. Ask yourself when you last used it. There will be oodles of things which have not seen the light of day in months, or even years - could you do without them?

And, remember this: in this day and age, one man's junk is another man's treasure! Online auction sites are easily accessible to all these days, and services are springing up all over, which make it easy to send items across the globe!

Your *5S SORT* may uncover goods which have a market value to someone else. It might be possible for you to get some money together, which you can use for small treats later, within your work.

SORT can also be a time to take a brave personal inventory. Ask yourself what negative habits you have accrued, which you could do with throwing away.

Allow yourself some time here; it can take months for something to become ingrained as a habit, and they are certainly challenging to break.

Maybe you could swap one for another. Stopping drinking can be tough, but if you combine it with an exercise regime, you will learn to associate not drinking with the increased feeling of wellbeing incurred from all those exercise endorphins.

At this early stage, when looking at yourself, get in the habit of writing things down. We will look at this in a little more detail later but, suffice to say, a thought is a fleeting thing; capture it and give it longevity! A small notebook would be an excellent investment to help you here.

I am going to finish talking about *SORT* by touching upon something a lot more complex: relationships.

When looking at ourselves and our personal habits, we also need to look at the relationships we have with others.

Undoubtedly, we all know incredibly negative people. Their presence can sometimes be draining, and your frequency will lower to theirs. There is seldom malice in the way that they are, but still you feel bad when you are around them. Ask what you can do to reduce the influence of this person on the way that you feel.

Your outlook is a vitally important factor in how you interact with the Universe. It has been said, very many times, in very many books, that you attract the things that you think about. This, in essence, is what this whole book is about: through the simple work of *5S*, you will make yourself feel better; less burdened by clutter; less bowed by those who love a good moan and a groan.

Have you ever noticed that pessimistic and negative people are seldom disappointed? That is because they have already decided the outcome of whatever event is in focus, before it even happens! Perhaps, in contrast, you also know one of those serenely positive people who glide through life, with seemingly no effort, and come up smelling of roses, every single time? Just as negativity breeds negativity, so positivity breeds positivity.

Your outlook, in every circumstance, is a matter of choice. Who you let into your life, and who and what you allow to influence you, is a matter of that very same choice.

There is so much truth in this statement that it should immediately make you sit up and think. Naturally, it may not be possible to simply "sort" all of the negative influences out of our life, but it is possible to reduce our exposure, or to change the way that we react. It must be said, though, that positive thought without affirmative action will not get you very far; you have to back up your convictions - almost like a gambler, going all-in on the turn of a card.

A simple set of actions, to get you underway, is to begin with *5S*, the foundation stone of all lean business – and, this starts with *SORT*.

SET

The second S is *SET*. In workplace *5S*, this means having a place for everything, and everything in its place. The idea is to put things where they are needed, so that you minimize wasted searching and movement. For instance, in the car industry, wasted operator motion is a cardinal sin; when someone is moving, they are not adding value to a vehicle. In the home, we don't need such vigour, but the general theory still holds.

One of the best things I ever did was to put a little hook

inside the front door of my home; I had used to spend ages looking for my keys! I would throw them down anywhere when I got in, and if I was a little worse for wear when that occurred, the keys could end up anywhere! But, with their storage location now set, I have never had to look for them since. The best-organized room in your house is most likely to be the kitchen. Are your drawers nicely segregated, with the forks in the fork section and the knives in with the knives? Woe betide any who tears this rule asunder and places a teaspoon where only the big spoons should go! This is an excellent example of *5S SET*. If you can apply this to your home, you will never have to look for anything again. Furthermore, it is a great motivator: you will need to correct anything that is out of place! In this way, you keep *SORT*-ing and preventing the clutter from ever reappearing; you are in control.

Part of using *SET* in a workplace is to define and label all storage locations. You can, of course, do this if you wish, but I suspect that may be a step too far. However, there is great logic to labelling.

Occasionally, I need to reboot my television box or internet router. The equipment is all plugged into the same power tower, along with a multitude of other electronic devices, so, when I need to unplug one, I am often left wondering which plug belongs to which device. If someone had their life-support machine drawing power from there, they would be in big trouble because, by this point, I am pulling out plugs, left, right and centre! What a difference a few stickers on the plugs would make! By the time this book is finished, I promise to have achieved this task – and, also to have attacked the snakes' nest of cords behind my toaster!

Returning to the workplace, what *SET* also achieves is to install "Kanban" pull signals. *Kanban* is another Japanese word: it means "flag". So, what does this mean?

Imagine I am working on a process, by which I fit screws to a part. I might use a two-bin system: two small bins of screws might sit on a shelf, which slopes slightly toward me. I am happily working away, using up the screws, when the stock in the first bin runs out. Not a problem: I remove the empty container, which means the second, full one behind it automatically slides forward. I now place the empty bin to the back and – and, here is the critical point - I set it on its backside, pointing upward. This is my Kanban pull signal: it is a clear visual indicator, to the line runner, that my empty consumables bin needs replenishing. As long as the process is observed, I will never run out of screws.

So, at home, I operate a two milk-carton system: I always have two cartons, so that when one runs out, I open the next. I place the old carton on the side, but it does not go into the recycling until a replacement has been entered onto the shopping list. This way, I never run out of milk. Gone are the late-night walks to the expensive convenience store! I actually find it pleasing to buy the milk I need before I need it.

SHINE

SHINE is the most misunderstood S within the *5S* methodology. I like to summarize it by the simple phrase "cleaning with meaning". In the workplace, this means that cleaning is deployed primarily as a form of inspection.

Let us discuss a practical example: imagine that you are washing your car - even I have been known to do this once or twice, but only on those special occasions when the windows are too dirty to see out of! As with cleaning any machine, I start at the top and work my way downward: there is little point washing the roof last, only to find that the runoff has dirtied the sides, which I so diligently polished earlier! It is only when washing the vehicle that I will see that little dent, or the small rust patch, or that tiny chip in my windscreen. At this point, I still have the opportunity to do something about them, before they become more significant problems. This is why I am "cleaning with meaning": I have the opportunity to fix issues prior to failure. In the workplace, this is fundamental. I would rather have a machine offline for a couple of hours, for a small repair, than wait the two weeks it takes for a new part and an available engineer, when it actually does go down!

Think about your car again. When you are cleaning it, is there the chance that you will check the water? Maybe you can check the washer bottles, the oil level and the tyre pressures at the same time. As the owner of the machine, you begin to take responsibility for the routine maintenance tasks. In the workplace, we call this "Autonomous Maintenance", and it is driven by the third step of *5S*: *SHINE.*

So, how is this applicable to your own life? On a material level, let's think about the biggest assets you own: these might well be your car and your home. We have already described cleaning the car - the same is true of your home. Notice a damp spot on the ceiling? Investigate now, before the water starts to drip through (I am familiar with this one, through personal experience and a wet head in the night)! You can save many thousands of pounds by carrying out these small maintenance tasks before they increase in size and complexity. Plus, the momentum makes you feel great! You'll begin to take on further maintenance and cleaning tasks; you'll become something of a human dynamo!

But, in terms of the way we live our life today, there are further aspects of *SHINE* which are worth exploring. Without a doubt, the most complex and remarkable machine we all own is the one which transports us, twenty-four hours a day: our body.

The human body is amazingly resilient, so there is never a wrong time to start maintaining it. Now, I am not going to say you must go to the gym every night and eat all the right foods – though, if this is where your momentum takes you, that would be fantastic.

Continuous Improvement is about small step changes. It is the logic which asks the question: "What small action am I going to do today?" Some Continuous Improvement practitioners call this *"Kata"* logic. Maybe it is about the fuel which goes into our machine? Perhaps it is dropping from two sweeteners to one in your coffee? Or, perhaps, replacing one of those coffees with water? Maybe it is getting off of the bus a stop earlier, and walking the rest of the way to work? Whatever it is, it needs to be small, it needs to be manageable, and it needs to be something which you can replicate, without breaking out into a cold sweat of dread and fear; remember, we are trying to build momentum. There are no timeframes at this point; you won't need to hold yourself accountable just yet, although that will inevitably need to follow.

In terms of *SHINE*, there is a great deal that we can do to clean the way we think. It took me a long time to realize that I had been thinking negatively for much, if not all, of my life - at least, until relatively recently. Why, then, should I be surprised that I had encountered so many difficult circumstances, prior to that point? It is worth considering that preceding line again: *I thought in a negative way and I received negative outcomes.* What might happen if I began to think in a positive way?

Hypochondria can be defined as a pre-occupying anxiety about your own health. Have you ever noticed that hypochondriacs are seldom at a loss for juicy details to share with you, about their state of wellbeing? Could it be that they are genuinely ill people? Could it be that they attract this ill health to themselves, via its being the primary pertaining line of their thinking? Therefore, could positive thinking really begin to attract positive circumstances into my life? I resolved to give it a try.

Now, I am going to be honest with you: after thirty to

forty years of negativity, the brain gets wired a certain way - like a radio pre-tuned to a particular station. You might be able to change it for a short while, but when that signal is lost, the radio quickly scans back to the previous frequency. This is where *SHINE* is particularly useful. In the workplace, we would always clean and inspect equipment before allowing it to be utilized - in the effort of applying Kaizen to your life, you need to start cleaning and inspecting the very thoughts which spring into your mind.

Again, let me be truthful: this is a tremendously difficult piece of work, particularly if, like me, you have allowed all negative thoughts free rein over the years, the majority being of no real value. I still find this very difficult to do, although there are times when I catch myself, at the beginning of an unwelcome thought: perhaps I am about to think that someone is stupid, or selfish, or some other cheap, throwaway slur. Then, I catch myself and I think: *No, I am not going to give that thought life!*

It comes with the realization that, in reality, there are very, very few genuinely bad people in the world - very few indeed. I like to think that most people in this life are just trying to do the very best that they can, with the circumstances and the information that they have, during the specific moment we encounter them. Does anyone really go out of their way to annoy us? Really? Even those of a fundamental nature are only, potentially, operating under the extreme notion that they are right.

The true freedom of thought begins when you start to accept that people view life differently to you. Social media is a case in point; there are few reasons why people share information this way. If I consider some of the content I have posted on social media in the past, I wonder what my motivation was in posting. By sharing information, was I trying to show that I was cleverer than others? Perhaps it was even to demonstrate that I was a better person; that I felt things more *correctly*. I had considered all of the nuances; I wasn't reactionary, but considered. Perhaps - and I think that this is the primary reason for most politically motivated posts that you see - I was right, and I had a moral duty to re-align the unfortunately flawed opinions of others? I wasn't preaching; I was helping (the irony being, of course, that this is exactly what I am doing here).

So, to return to the original point: be careful what you allow into your head and be careful what you allow out. You must be vigilant at every moment of every day, and it is tough. This has been written many times before, by people much wiser than me.

What you think about, you tend to attract toward you.

Let's face it explicitly: we are describing the *Law of Attraction.*

Now, whilst there is a lot to admire about the Law of Attraction, similarly to *5S* Workplace Organization, it appears to be open to misinterpretation and misunderstanding. *5S* Workplace Organization cannot function without action – and, it is exactly the same for the Law of Attraction. Holding a vision of something in your mind won't work, without carrying out a set of actions required to bring that objective to fruition. When we *SHINE* our thoughts, to be vigilant for those periods of negativity, we must follow up with action, no matter how small. This is what Napoleon Hill termed as "applied faith": you have set the objective, now do you have the faith to back your bet?

STANDARDIZE

When we apply the *STANDARDIZE* step of *5S* in a workplace, we set out to do one thing: the rationale of *STANDARDIZE* is to communicate to everyone in the area what "good" looks like.

In practice, the easiest way to do this is to display a

photograph of the optimum condition in the work area. This means that any deviations from the standard are a) instantly recognizable and b) can then be aligned with the standard.

In terms of our own *5S*, it may not be absolutely necessary to have a visual standard of what a tidy kitchen looks like - that is, unless you live with some particularly messy people (I do, and it is me!) - but, it doesn't hurt to have a visual indicator of what you are aiming for, at the commencement of your improvement journey. Maybe you could find a picture of your favourite holiday destination or your dream car? Those more expert in the Law of Attraction than myself describe this as a "vision board", though I wonder about the applicability of envisioning mansions and expensive motor cars with a journey of Continuous Improvement. These outcomes might very well manifest themselves eventually, but the idea and purpose of this book is to think about starting small and building toward that eventual snowball momentum. So, perhaps we need to swap the sports car for a new pair of swish shoes, and the private jet for a top of the range television. The things you hope to achieve should be just out of reach, but not a lifetime away.

Next, you would commit to bringing those images into

your mind as often as you can. Visualize yourself in the new car; hear the engine roar, as you push down on the accelerator; smell the leather of the interior; feel the force on your body, as the vehicle effortlessly sweeps around a sunlit, sea-scented bend; feel the excitement, the adrenalin, then bring the vehicle to a serene stop and give gratitude for being blessed by owning it.

When you are next doing the washing-up, use the time to repeat affirmations relating to your purpose in life. Ensure that the affirmations are rooted in the present: "I *am* financially abundant", not "I *will be* financially abundant". Can you see the difference? Feel the gratitude for the money (or the point of your focus) and repeat. This is *5S STANDARDIZE*: helping your mind understand what "good" feels like. and the situation that it needs to work toward.

SUSTAIN

The final step of Workplace Organization is *SUSTAIN*. Some systems call this "Self Discipline", or "Stick", which gives you an idea of what it is all about.

It may also give you some inkling that sustaining the

condition of a workplace or a home is a difficult thing to do: one moment of non-vigilance could see you regress, significantly. This is why the *SUSTAIN* step is so vital and so tricky. In the workplace, it is common to see this step being managed by an audit system, which would score the area under review against assessment criteria across the *5S* categories; incremental target scores would be agreed, perhaps with small rewards given for attaining and, more importantly, maintaining a score, before the target was reset. There is nothing stopping you from designing and carrying out your own audit, but this may prove to be rather onerous in the long-term.

I would perhaps suggest a moment of reflection on how everything is going to this point. If things are not going too well, let me share the following with you:

Keypoint:
There is nothing wrong with failing, as long as you learn and try again.

This is an exceptionally important point. Read it again and let it sink in; it will be a common theme of everything we will explore together in this book.

Nobody was ever successful by giving up, and nobody who was ever successful got it right the first time. Here in the U.K., there is a brand of lubricant called "WD40" - the WD stands for the words "water displacement", but the real story lies in the number: it is simply the fortieth recipe that the developers tried; there were thirty-nine previously unsuccessful formulas! Each time around the buoy, each iteration gave them something new, and finally there was no choice but to get it right.

So, if you look at your *5S* efforts and you are not overly impressed, don't worry; learn from where you are and recommence your efforts. Challenge yourself: what one small thing are you going to improve today? If it is tackling that ironing pile, let it be that. Let every step be a step towards something worthwhile.

The main thing to say about the *SUSTAIN* step is that it should lead to a Continuous Improvement action plan – otherwise, the efforts become stale, and all improvement is lost. Action is key.

Keypoint:

What one small thing am I going to improve today?

In practice, *5S* Workplace Organization is a holistic piece of work, and the steps are often carried out simultaneously. Tools which are deemed to be necessary are cleaned and inspected, then stored in their designated location. The thing which makes *5S* so successful is embedded action. What I mean by that is that the steps above - *SORT, SET, SHINE, STANDARDIZE* and *SUSTAIN* - become so ingrained into everyday activity that they become habit.

Twelve-step addiction programmes recognize this very well; they ask you to give them ninety days: this is the amount of time it is thought is needed for repeated activity to become a habit. Whether these are positive or negative habits, the brain and the Universe do not distinguish, and addressing a lousy habit within oneself often requires a seismic shock to the system. I probably knew that I was a problem gambler for a long time, but I did not have the will to address it until everything was gone, by which point it was far too late. Now, ten years on, it is a habit not to gamble, though I keep the memory of that person with me at all times, as a reminder of how far I am blessed to have come. This is why I am happy to recommend starting with the smallest of actions.

As the days pass, your momentum will become fortified

by the power of habit, which in turn will give you the strength to set yourself ever-increasing targets which, in themselves, will become ever more achievable.

It is a lot like going to the gym. On the first day, I lift the smallest weights; a few weeks later, these will have become too light, and I move on to something heavier. By the end of the year, I have become transformed: I am fitter, stronger and leaner, and have bundles of energy to address the improvements that I would like to make in this life.

Your life can be like that in every area of your efforts; whether it be at home, work or socially, it can all start with the five small steps of Workplace Organization.

3

THE PDCA CYCLE

Let us now add a little more structure and think about the "PDCA Cycle". In the world of business improvement, this is a methodology to manage the small step changes which we strive for, in a Continuous Improvement environment. It is a highly effective yet simple structure which, when used wholly and correctly, gives solid, sustainable results.

PLAN –DO – CHECK – ACT.

That is all the PDCA Cycle stands for: a simple strategy. Let's first look at the parts, then at the whole.

PLAN

The first stage is when we *PLAN.*

Whether this is in the workplace or applied to our

personal lives, the step begins in the same way: we arrive at a situation whereby we need to improve something.

In terms of problem-solving, the first requirement is to detect the problem. Not to define it - which we will come to later - but to actually detect it, understand that it is present and accept it. In the business environment, this can be difficult, as you may need to align many people and convince them to place their hands on their heart and accept what you are saying.

Most of the stress we endure, either at work or at home, is a direct result of our own resistance to the situation in which we find ourselves - only by accepting the current condition can we hope to change it. Don't get me wrong: we are definitely not talking here about a passive acceptance of the circumstances in our life - most certainly not; what we are saying is that acceptance is a healthy first step. It means that we have detected the problem. And, what is more, this acknowledgement of what *is* enables us to free up the energy which we have used worrying or stressing about it. We can then redirect that same energy in a much more positive way; the energy is used to create that urgency and impetus to change. How great it can feel to harness that positivity during the *PLAN* stage! At this point, you can start to define the situation you wish to change.

To do this, we need to capture a picture of the current moment, accurately. Think about writing a problem statement: what is the condition that you want to improve? In the workplace, you would probably go on to state how big the problem is. Where is it detected? How is it detected? What is its deviation from the standard? Does the problem occur during a particular cycle? How often does it occur? Do we know where it occurs? When we apply the same rigour to our own situation, the chances are we will have a feel for these or similar questions. The key point here is to write something down and make it emotive.

Let's think about what a problem statement might look like in terms of losing weight:

"During 2019, I weighed approximately 20lbs over my optimum. This led to occasions of depression, lack of energy and ill-discipline in my eating/drinking habits."

What do you think of the above as a problem statement? It tells us what the problem is (being overweight); when it occurred (2019); and, the deviation from standard (20lbs). It also tells us how that problem *impacts* us: through depression and poor nutrition - it is the impact part of the statement which we are looking to solve.

The next stage of the *PLAN* activity is to measure the current situation. I am going to map this against a classic quality, cost and delivery model, just so that you can see:

Quality: *deviation from standard weight of 20lbs; current weight 200lbs.*

Cost: *over the last six months, approximately £200 spent on junk food; approximately £800 spent on alcohol; £180 spent on gym membership.*

Delivery: *attended the gym on zero occasions in the last six months (see above).*

Looking at the above metrics, it appears there is ample opportunity for improvement; even cancelling the unused gym membership would save money. But, is that a good outcome? Now might be an excellent time to set some targets.

But, first a word on target setting - this is a tricky area. It is, of course, possible to go a little easy at this stage and set yourself an eminently achievable target. This is not a good idea though, as it can stop your momentum in its tracks; the trouble with an easy target is that it can invoke the *"I'll start tomorrow"* approach. If something is easy, you have failed to apply the first step of the change model: i.e. to create the urgency for change.

On the other hand, an overly ambitious target can have much the same effect: *"There is no real point in starting this; it is realistically too difficult!"* Only you will know your threshold to set the goal.

There is nothing to say that you can't set incremental targets. When giving up gambling, I used the mantra *"just for today"*: *"Just for today, I will not have a bet."* Actually, the whole saying went something like this: *"Just for today, I will not have a bet. I might have one tomorrow, but I won't have one today."*

With any luck, you have already gained strength from your Workplace Organization efforts and have achieved some small victories there.

So, back to our goal-setting:

Target: *to lose 14lbs in the next three months (add an exact date here).*

DO

The *DO* phase is where you roll your sleeves up and get on with it!

Nobody became a published author without writing a book; nobody set up a successful business without having a product or service to sell; nobody ever solved a business problem without devising and trialling solutions; nobody ever, ever, ever willed themselves to get fit by mind-power alone.

Although, by its nature, this section will be relatively short, its importance cannot be underestimated. Kaizen, or Continuous Improvement - call it what you will - is a philosophy of *doing*! If you're waiting to win a lottery by visualizing millions of pounds, the chances are that you are going to have a long wait! Do, do, do!

But, remember, Rome wasn't built in a day! Small improvements and daily progress are where we need to be. If you haven't run for years, you wouldn't expect to go out and cover a marathon tomorrow! It might take you a couple of years to build up to any real distance. Set those incremental targets: *"I want to be able to run two miles in one month"*, or even *"I want to be able to run one mile in two weeks"*. Whatever you do, just do.

If you are working toward incremental targets, remember to build in positive reward systems. Let's say that I want to write the first draft of a new novel; I know I have to write roughly 80,000 words. How might I approach that? Well, from experience I know that, even on the busiest days, writing 500 words is achievable; it therefore follows that it will take 160 days, at 500 words a day, to complete my target.

In the manufacturing world, this is called my "Takt" time. *Takt* is a German word, which literally means "beat": the heartbeat of a process. Takt time is vitally important to planners, in order to work out if something is possible under the current condition, or whether additional resources need to be allocated. If I need to build 4000 computers, to meet an order, in five eight-hour days, then I need to build 100 computers per hour. By measuring the cycle time, I can then make a comparison.

Imagine that I have twenty cells, each contributing a process to the final computer, and I know that every 3600 seconds I need to push 100 computers through the line: theoretically, then, each cell must complete its process in 72 seconds - the moment one of my cells cannot achieve this, I cannot meet my customer order without additional resources or expensive overtime.

The reason I mention this point is to give you some idea of how to break down your overall objective. It may be that the final goal, whilst achievable, is still some way off. This is why celebrating your ongoing success is vital.

Remember that 500 words per day target I set for my 80,000-word novel? Well, in this age of digital television, I don't watch many T.V. programmes when they are actually broadcast; I prefer to watch a few, select shows that I like (typically comedies, because laughter is such a wonderful thing) on catch-up, at my leisure. So, there we have a wonderful reward system: I want to watch a particular show - well, of course I can, but I must write my 500 words first! Isn't that simply the same way that you might persuade a child to do homework?

So, start doing, and celebrate those small wins.

CHECK

During the *CHECK* phase of an improvement round, we typically ask ourselves one question: "Did the improvement work?"

Remember that we talked about measuring your starting point, during the *PLAN* section? This measure now becomes our comparator: did we meet the small target which we set ourselves, back at the beginning?

Keypoint:
Failure is not the end of the world!

There are two types of people in this world, but both types have something in common. Do you recognize these people: the majority of us, who get through life as if wading through treacle? Similarly, do you know that annoying someone for whom everything always works out; those who seem to glide through life, having everything fall in their lap? Do you want to be more like them? The similarity between these two groups of people is that both fail. The difference – and, I'm sure you are already ahead of me here - is the way that those people react to the failure, when it happens. The first group of people - who tend to be in the majority - see failure as an endpoint. In fact, they often probably expect it at the outset, so is it any wonder that they draw failure toward them? Most of their stories of endeavour begin: "I tried it once", or "I used to..." but, at the first sign of adversity, the towel comes flying in.

Keypoint:

The people who achieve success are no different to you!

Read that once more:

The people who achieve success are no different to you.

No different to most, in fact... except in one key area: they welcome failure.

As with many things in Continuous Improvement, and life in general, this seems counterintuitive, but it is absolutely necessary. Nearly every successful person can share stories of failed attempts and journeys full of struggle. But, every iteration of the PDCA Cycle is a wonderful opportunity to learn: *I had a plan, to achieve something; I did the "do", trialling my ideas, approaches, strategies and solutions; I stop for a check of my interim target: I have not quite made it.*

What do I do now? Do I throw up my hands, claim that this task is too difficult and consign it to history? No!!! No, I do not! I go back to the *PLAN* stage of the PDCA Cycle, and I ask myself: "What did I learn on the last iteration? What am I going to do differently, this time around?" This is why the small targets are so vitally important: I want to know if I am off-track quickly, so that I can return to my plan and tweak it where necessary. I don't want to find out a year from now that I haven't saved enough money for that holiday, or lost enough weight to buy that dream dress.

Set your Takt, set your milestones, keep checking and keep learning. The PDCA Cycle has been successfully applied in businesses across the globe, for decades, so there must be something in it.

Something that the most successful companies have in common is their desire to become what they term as "learning organizations". They learn through structured doing, and this learning is not confined to pockets of experts and strategists; it stretches throughout the business, most importantly reaching the real heroes of the piece: those on the front line, doing the value-added work; the people who realize the product or the service. A learning organization wants these heroes to drive the business forward - after all, they are the closest to the potential; everyone else in the enterprise exists purely to guide these people.

As individuals, surely, we have a much more dynamic opportunity: we own the entire vehicle and super-computer, and we can choose the energy and fuel that we decide to let in.

So, when you fail – and, you will - let the *CHECK* phase of the PDCA Cycle be a catalyst, to spur you on to greater efforts. Return to the *PLAN* phase, identify the improvement opportunity, and return with even more gusto.

The *CHECK* phase is also a good opportunity to take a second, sit back (enjoy the simple sunshine or the birds singing) and reflect on what you have done, and what you still have to do. The Japanese call this *"Hansei"*, a concept which we will discuss in more detail, later. Take a second to enjoy the now, and give gratitude for everything that you have. It may sound like a cliché, but no matter what our own life feels like, there are probably hundreds of people who would happily swap places with us. Gratitude is the key, and it feels good to give it.

ACT

If I had been looking at a business process, my journey to this point would look like this: I began with a *PLAN* for something that I wanted to fix or change; I would have assembled a cross-functional team, comprising of both expert and fresh eye perspectives; I would have gathered all of the pertinent information, relating to the current state; and, I would have analyzed that, to reach the root cause or causes. Next, I would have planned my solutions, before moving into the *DO* phase and trialling them, as per my action plan. My next step would have been to *CHECK* if the improvement has worked: was the quality of the process better than when I first measured it, during the *PLAN* phase? Perhaps I have removed some waste and decreased my cycle time? Perhaps I reassessed during the *CHECK* stage and found that I had made no discernible difference? Remember, this is not a problem: I would simply have returned to the *PLAN* phase, where I would choose to address a different root cause, or to deploy a different trial. Then, I would deploy the new trial and proceed, for the second time, onto the *CHECK* phase. Upon re-measuring, I would discover that I had achieved a success: my quality metric was better! Perhaps it was still not perfect, but there was clear evidence to suggest that I had made a significant step forward. Now is the time for the *ACT* phase.

ACT is a vitally important piece to the cycle, yet if there is one piece that businesses and change agents forget to implement, this can be it. *ACT* has two major applications with our business improvement method.

First, it helps the improvement to stick. If I have found a more productive way of working, then I need to ensure that I don't, through habit, revert to my old practices. I also need to be sure that those around me are aware of the change that I have made, and don't carry on doing what we were always doing, with exactly the same results.

So, for a business process improvement, I need to do a number of things: firstly, I need to document the change. This will most probably mean updating a document, such as a "Standard Operating Procedure", or an "Engineering Standard". Once updated, I then have to train my change out to those individuals who are going to be charged with implementing and maintaining it. With any luck, these people were heavily involved in the improvement process anyway, so they are already bought into the change and thoroughly understand the need for its implementation. If not, I might have a difficult sales job on my hands! Once the training begins, I will need to ensure that I have a mechanism for recording this. This will principally be the "Skills Matrix": the document which describes who in your area can do what, and to what level of competence they can achieve it. This can be a very useful document, indeed: there is no way that you want to authorize holiday for Bob and Dave during the same week, if they are the only two people trained to carry out a critical task!

The second aspect of the *ACT* phase is of vital importance. Remember, the *ACT* phase should cement the new improvement, and will hopefully level out performance at the new augmented standard. Enjoy the moment, by all means, but understand one thing: this new level becomes the jumping-off point for your next improvement!

Keypoint:

The new level becomes the jumping-off point for your next improvement.

Do you see what this infers? Where does this realization naturally send you in the PDCA Cycle? That's right: back to the *PLAN* phase, ready to start a whole new improvement cycle, with more challenging targets. It is this step which makes your efforts continuous - which take you that step nearer to the ideal. Business improvement professionals can be fond of the odd cliché (as you will already have seen from this book), but none are wasteful or trite: Kaizen is a journey, not a destination.

Take a look at the following number sequence:

$$1 + \frac{1}{2} + \frac{1}{4} + \frac{1}{8} + \frac{1}{16} + \frac{1}{32} + ...$$

Every addition adds a sum which takes us from 1 toward a total of 2, but... it is impossible for it to ever get there! It will, however, get us closer and closer and closer, each time. Each addition can be thought of as a metaphor for the PDCA

Cycle – a cycle of which you are now fully aware and a relative expert.

So now, from a personal perspective, what is the *ACT* phase telling us? Primarily, I think it is that we need to make our "good" behaviour our standard behaviour. We can only achieve this through habit, and small successes can only serve to embed that habit with meaning and positivity. Secondly, when we achieve a target, remember that that is only one step. Yes, we can celebrate; yes, we can reflect; but, again, the habit of momentum should lead us to return to the plan and re-tweak our targets, so that we can set off on the next stage of our transformative journey.

The PDCA Cycle is the structure behind our new mindset. We are not here to fix the world, but we are here to implement a series of positive Kaizen step changes which, as a whole, will gather momentum and impact with impressive speed.

FURTHER DISCUSSION POINTS RELATING TO PDCA

Generally, within the planning phase of a small Kaizen

project, you would assemble a team to work together. Ideally, you would want your team to be drawn from across your business, not just the area where the problem occurs; it is often those team members with the least knowledge about a process who can provide the breakthrough. They are going to present the challenge with *"why?"* and their fresh-eyed approach can often inspire fresh thinking amongst the experts of the team - those traditionally too close to the problem to see the solution.

The team which we are describing here will need certain environmental advantages to help them prosper; their success will hinge upon how well they can draw forth the knowledge and experience of everybody within the group. If the team contains a dominant individual, behind whom everyone follows then, in reality, the group are only drawing upon the much more limited resource of that one individual. What is even worse is when there are one or two negative people within the team. Perhaps they think that the problem is unsolvable, so there is no real reason to begin working on it; they often have that *"Kaizen won't work here"* mentality. Usually, these are long-serving members of the workforce, who have seen it all, done it all and long since thrown out the proverbial t-shirt. What is unlikely, though, is that co-workers such as these have always had this frame of mind; rounds of failed campaigns, poor communication and broken promises have taken their toll, so their views have become jaded and disconnected from the overall vision.

If some of this is feeling familiar, it is because it occurs everywhere. You may even be starting to recognize yourself in this description. If you have taken the next step and are already pondering how this might relate to your personal journey, then your thinking is already showing signs of greater clarity, because this description of tired colleagues relates to your own private activities, and very importantly so: your negative team members may be equally negative people within your own life. We spoke about this earlier, but it is well worth returning to this broader context; we have discussed the need to be cautious around the negative people in your life - they are there, this much is almost certainly true.

But, let's think now about how we might assemble a more positive support group, to sustain us through the PDCA iterations. A group of positive people bounces off of each other, and they encourage their peers to more considerable efforts. Not much of a revelation, is it? The additional bonus of this fact is that this group do not all have to be necessarily working toward the same thing: it is the support which counts; that one person who becomes your conscience, and offers that little bit of accountability. "Bob, did you go to the gym today?" asks Gina. Bob sighs; *I'd better go to the gym today; Gina will only keep asking!* This is why fellowships which support the sufferers of addiction work so well: letting yourself down is often more palatable than letting down a perfect stranger.

However, if you cannot, at this moment, envisage building a support group of mutually encouraging buddies, please do not despair. The internet is full of videos which offer a myriad of uplifting messages and thoughts; it might even be that you listen to an uplifting song or watch a favourite comedy clip. Maybe you could find an online group to join. If not, why not be the one to reach out, take the initiative and start one? Build that team, either in reality or virtually.

The great Napoleon Hill likened the mind to a garden spot: you have to be careful what you plant there, and what you use to nourish the soil and plants - a further thought to consider. Be careful with whom you share your purpose. I know this is overwhelmingly tempting, particularly when you have just started out, or are making good progress, but sometimes discretion is called for. Not everybody will share your vision, and some may deride or even look to derail your efforts. In some circles, success is still seen as something vulgar, or portrayed as a betrayal of your roots. You and I know that this is ridiculous, but beware that this view is not always shared; *"What gives you the right to expect any more than the rest of us?"* So, be careful about sharing your new success consciousness.

This is where your success support group can come in – but, beware of comparing with them, too.

Go at your own pace, and remember that the key is to filter out all negative outside influences: even a comment given in jest could rock your confidence and slow your momentum.

4

THE THREE DIVISIONS OF WORK

In moving on to our next topic, we must first stop and examine the three divisions of work.

First, let's start by mentally picturing a timeline. At one end, I have a pile of parts and components - perhaps they are the pieces needed to build a laptop computer; at the other end of the timeline, there is the finished piece of equipment. As the laptop shell passes along the line, the components required are fitted and assembled. As we know, the output required of this process is the completed, operational machine, which is something that the customer wants and is happy to pay for. It therefore follows that any process step I undertake, which brings that pile of parts one step nearer to becoming the completed laptop (assembling and fitting the motherboard, for example), is also something that the customer is willing to pay for. These steps are what we call "value-added".

Occasionally, my mythical computer may stop along my production line, to be inspected or have a component scanned from inventory; maybe it is to have an electrical test, required by law, to allow the finished item to be sold in a particular country. Whilst none of these steps bring the computer any closer to being built, they are necessary to the process - I am going to use the term "non-value-added" to describe these steps. If you work in Continuous Improvement for any given time, you will undoubtedly hear other terms, but "non-value-added" is as good as any.

So, we have defined the value-added and non-value-added steps within our manufacturing process, but there is one destructive group left - which we define as "waste".

5

THE EIGHT WASTES

In manufacturing (and indeed across all industries), we typically define eight classic wastes. I shall describe them here, using one of the many mnemonics which can be applied: *"TIMWOODS"*.

TRANSPORTATION

Typically described as the unnecessary movement of goods and materials, This is very common in older factories, where the layout was not necessarily designed to support modern processes.

One sign that a business is suffering from transportation waste is the presence of fleets of forklift trucks, enclosed by crash barriers. Applying *5S*, particularly *SET*, is one way of beginning to combat this waste: e.g. by bringing related processes closer together.

In terms of our own lives, it may be that we temporarily

store things, moving them twice, instead of once. Perhaps we have a pile of clean washing which gets moved around and never gets ironed.

INVENTORY

Holding too much raw material and stock is quite a tricky waste, and can hurt a business in many ways. Firstly, money tied up in inventory is dead money; you have paid for it, but it is not earning you anything. Secondly, you are paying to store it, most likely in a building which is heated and lit, and may even be incurring the expense of rental. Thirdly, there is the danger of obsolescence; items which are being stored might expire before they are ever used. This is often the case when a business buys the same order of something - a chemical, say - month after month. The original order is never challenged and yet, strangely, the company disposes of quantities of the same chemical, month after month after month. Before you know it, you have run out of storage space and things are being stored in temporary locations. But, guess what: this leads to an increase in transportation, at best. At worst, items which are on-site somewhere get lost, and expensive replacements are expedited from the supplier, even though the original product was there all along.

The ideal, of course, is *"just in time (JIT)"* replenishment. Here, items are replaced just as they are used up. A production line might signal that it needs something, and it is replenished just before it runs out. This request is an example of a pull signal - as we have already seen, the trigger for this pull signal is known by the Japanese word "Kanban". Naturally, this is equally applicable to our own lives. We all know someone who has enough food and groceries crammed into their cupboards, fridges and freezers to supply a small army for several weeks. This is just inventory waste on a smaller scale. We are creatures of habit; we go to the supermarket and pick up all the same items, through no more than habit, whether we need them or not. These items then get put right at the front of the larder or storage cupboard - and, we now have a problem: when looking for a tin, for example, we will probably pick the first one on the shelf, especially if we are in a hurry. This tin was the one which went in last; we have now created a *"FISH"* situation: *"First in, still here!"*

What we are actually hoping for is *"FIFO": "First in, first out."* If you think about a fast-food restaurant, the burgers are loaded from the back of the service area and slide forward. This ensures that the picker always has to take the oldest burger first. In fact, the next stage is applied, too: where minimal amounts of each burger are stored in each chute. Replenishments are initiated directly by customer order - the ultimate pull system.

MOTION

Motion is defined as the unnecessary movement of people within the workspace. This is a simple one to spot, but it can be more challenging to solve.

In the car industry, there is an aspiration to have all parts and tooling within one metre of the point of fit. It stands to reason that you do not want your skilled operative traipsing halfway down the plant to find a part. But, this is also true on a much smaller scale: you also don't want them eating up seconds by stretching or twisting for something. Nor do you want them injured, as they carry out these unergonomic movements, hundreds, if not thousands of times a day. A whole science has arisen out of the requirement to give operators everything they need, in precisely the place they need it, and at the correct orientation. If this sounds like the objective of a *5S SORT* and *SET*, it is because these two steps of Workplace Organization are the primary tools to be deployed in the pursuit of the ergonomic workplace, and the elimination of motion waste.

When I sit down to do some writing, I make sure that everything I need is at hand. If I need to get up to find a notebook or a pencil, to plug in my laptop charger, or whatever else it might be, I know that these are the times when I am most likely to become distracted from my value-adding task. Perhaps I'll decide to put some laundry on - a task which needs to be done, yes, but is non-value-adding, nonetheless, in terms of my primary purpose. Likewise, if I am typing away whilst sitting on the sofa, I had better make sure that the television remotes are out of reach! *"I'll just watch ... for ten minutes..."* is the point at which many dreams falter!

So, I guess the overarching message here is: be *doing* what you are doing; try to avoid "mental motion". Be exercising when you are exercising; be writing when you are writing; be vacuuming when you are vacuuming. Live in the now, plan and stick to it. If you manage that, reward yourself with something frivolous.

WAITING

This is when a process stops... then waits for something to happen, in order to allow it to restart. Maybe this something is an inspection, a machine changeover, or even just a signature. Whatever it is, it is time which is ticking away.

In our own lives, one of the biggest waiting wastes is one of the easiest to address. Imagine the following scenario: it's October, and I am feeling a little sluggish; I know I have put on a few pounds. I need to go on a diet or, better still, do some exercise. But, then I take a look at the calendar and say to myself: "Well, it's going to be Christmas in a couple of months, so it isn't worth starting an exercise regime before then! I'll start in the New Year, when the party season is over." Then, January comes and goes... "I'll start in March, when the weather starts getting a little warmer..." You get the idea.

So many of us spend our lives waiting for the perfect time to start something but, deep down, we all know the simple truth: there is never a perfect time to start any endeavour. Start where you stand. Challenge yourself with the question: "What one thing can I do today?"

OVER-PRODUCTION

This applies when making too many of something, or making them too fast.

If I only have orders to make 10,000 laptop computers, and I make 20,000, then what am I to do with the remaining 10,000 surplus items? In reality, I will have to push them onto the market and hope that someone eventually buys them. Imagine trying to push a length of rope: it is just going to end up in a heap! On the other hand, if I have orders for 10,000 and I make 10,000, I can almost imagine my customers lining up by a conveyor at my door, pulling the computers from the line. Additionally, if I exceed this order, by the time the surplus stock begins to sell, a competitor might have already launched a new, quicker machine, making my excess effectively obsolete.

As you can see, if I have an imperfect process (doesn't everyone?) which has wastes along the line, every one of those wastes becomes magnified, as more and more iterations of that cycle are applied. In terms of our Continuous Improvement efforts in our own lives, I think this would most accurately translate as *"keep to your planned pace"*. It is the tortoise versus the hare concept.

I imagine that you can call to mind many occasions in

the past when you have endeavoured to do something - perhaps it is a new hobby or a diet. Let's say I decide to join a gym. On the first day, I go along and I train for three hours straight - for the following week, my whole body is wracked with pain and covered with bruises; my resolve is broken. All of that new gym kit I bought gets thrown into the back of the closet and forgotten about, forever associated with the torture I put myself through in the violent crucible of the weight-benches. All because I went off at a pace which was damaging and unsustainable.

OVER-PROCESSING

Doing more than that which is needed to complete a job or meet a customer requirement - this is a waste I have seen several times, in different businesses.

Let us imagine that we have a clear customer specification, which informs the "Upper Control Limit" and "Lower Control Limit" (*UCL* and *LCL*) of our process. Perhaps we are manufacturing a pin, which can be between 500 and 750 microns in diameter (a micron is 1/1000th of a millimetre) - this we can achieve fairly well, but in fact we decide only to accept pins between 575 and 675 microns in diameter. This causes our cycle time to increase and also causes us to scrap or rework pins which fall outside of our range. Clearly, we are over-processing here; we are doing more work than the customer requires and, what is more, we are not getting paid for it. The difficulty comes because, when we have provided this tighter service once, our customer is probably going to expect it again, when something machined with a greater tolerance would still be perfectly acceptable.

So, what might the life-based application of over-processing be? If we use the definition of *"doing more for a task than you need to do"*, we may well see where the similarities lie.

In the past, I have attempted to write novels. The accepted route to market with most books is to find an agent, who is willing to represent you. The difficulty comes in finding the point when you are confident enough to put your work out there; the overwhelming temptation is to keep amending your manuscript. The danger here is that we get so bogged down in looking for a level of perfection which we cannot achieve, we never make that leap of faith.

Another way to look at it might be that you like a sport – running, perhaps; you have been training for a while, and you are getting fitter, but you still worry about being too slow to enter a local race. You don't enter and, eventually, your enthusiasm wanes; you missed the chance, waiting for the perfect time! Perfect times never come. Start from where you are today.

DEFECTS

Items which are not right the first time are either scrapped or reworked. These items have a cost to the business, both in scrap and in the amount of time which was utilized to add the value the product has gained so far. The later in the process that the defect impacts, the greater the cost of the rework or, in extreme cases, the scrap of the entire product.

If you were to question most people about waste in business, particularly in the manufacturing sector, the chances are that defects would be the first thing they would mention. After all, there is not much on a workshop floor more unsightly than a bulging scrap bin.

For our thinking, I am going to spin this a little. Imagine that we are manufacturing an expensive automobile. We realize that that the chassis and engine are both failed units, but we keep on building, adding extra parts, extra value and extra time. The outcome will still be the same: we are going to get a scrap car. Surely, the sense in this situation is to recognize when we should cut our losses and start building a new car! I come back to this point again: failure is not the end of the world, as long as you learn and are willing to start again.

When I was younger, I wanted to be a professional darts player. The trouble was that I wasn't any good. No amount of positive visualization and practice was going to change that; even though I spent years attempting to improve, I just couldn't get past a certain level. The truth is that most professional darts players are outstanding from the first time they pick up a dart. Either that, or they have the drive to practice for six or seven hours a day. I had neither the natural talent nor the extreme drive to be successful - it was clearly time for me to try something else. Unfortunately, another disaster - more expensive in so many ways — followed: I became caught up with the idea of being a professional gambler. It was a habit which took me another fifteen years to finally kick, and only then because there was no other choice.

SKILLS AND SUGGESTIONS

Not utilizing the skills of your people effectively, and ignoring their improvement suggestions, is the eighth waste, but it wasn't always deemed so. In years gone by, experts recognized seven wastes within manufacturing – then, rightly so, the misuse of the skills and suggestions of a business's people was added.

There are a number of things which any business endeavour cannot exist without, and the goodwill of staff is certainly amongst them. What this waste also recognizes is that the best people to improve any process are those who know it the best: i.e. those who actually do the work. True, they may sometimes need someone with a fresh-eyed approach, to challenge and ask the question *"why?"* but, at the end of the day, their knowledge will find a knack or a method to make the job easier. It is no longer enough to have a cadre of "experts" remotely managing improvements from a distant office; it must be done at the *"gemba"* - the coal face, where the work actually gets done.

So, as we seek to find improvement in our own circumstances, by all means we can read books, watch videos and gain know-how from those who have been there before us but, in the final analysis, we must do the work ourselves, at our own *gemba*, as we all know the way we ourselves operate. Ultimately, however, we need to be truthful to ourselves, and while it is unrealistic to expect immediate perfection, we must also be aware of the wastes in our own improvement processes, which could slow or even halt our progress. Perhaps it is apt to think about being the tortoise rather than the hare.

The Japanese refer collectively to the wastes described above as *"muda"*. But, they are only a fraction of the problem.

It is worth thinking about another two concerns here; in truth, we face a trio of interlinked foes. But, daunting as it sounds, awareness is half the battle, so let us demystify things even further.

"Mura" can be thought of as unevenness. In business, this can be quite destructive. Where workload is uneven, processes and people can experience a feast or famine environment. Quiet times are okay for a short while, but if you have ever been at work for an extended period, when there is not much to do, you will realize just how demotivating and depressing that circumstance can be. Then, all of a sudden, bang! A huge order comes in, and it

is all hands to the pump. To instantaneously change from a slow walk to a full sprint is tremendously difficult to do: expensive overtime ensues and supply lines are sucked dry, and begin to struggle. It is then that we encounter our third category of peril: *"muri"*. *Muri* means "overburden".

Because the work is compressing into this new peak, people and machines become overburdened; in both cases, the outcome is the same: breakdown. Machines begin to malfunction, causing downtime. This means that the available time becomes more compressed and increases the burden on the machine, which, in turn, increases the unevenness of the process. People then start rushing - they make more mistakes, which reduces yield and creates more rework, which in turn creates more overburden. People become more rushed; some start to break down and absenteeism rises, which cranks up the pressure on those remaining, which increases the unevenness, which creates more defects, which increases the overburden, which drives up the unevenness, and so on... ad infinitum, until criticality is reached. Wouldn't it be better to have that work spread out smoothly across the year, so that all are nicely, sustainably busy all of the time?

You can probably already see how this applies to our efforts to Kaizen our lives. The evidence can be seen every

January, in every gym across the developed world. They are the bane of the regular member's life, but the enthused New Year exercise fanatic generally doesn't last that long. Why? Well, deep down we all know why: either we expect too much too soon and become demoralized by the lack of stunning results, or we go mad for the first couple of days and end up in so much pain that our zeal quickly dissipates, and our gym pass becomes just another card on the side. That is actually the business model of a gym: sign up three or four times the number of members that you need, because most of them will never come anyway, but will continue to pay the membership fee, just in case. How do I know this? Well, it is not by owning a gym!

So, slow and steady wins the race. Consistent, daily effort toward our planned outcomes will always be more productive than pockets of uncontrolled, exhausting and frenzied activity. Guess what? The Japanese have a name for this, too: they call it *"heijunka"*, or "level-loading", where we can enjoy predictability, flexibility and stability.

6

VISUAL MANAGEMENT

The fourth of the *5S* is *STANDARDIZE*: e.g. help everyone to understand what "good" looks like. It is this S which drives "Visual Management" within the workplace and guides us toward the goal of the visual business.

So, what do we mean when we talk of a visual business? Essentially, we are describing a work environment which adequately supports the standard work to be carried out. Furthermore, the visual workplace lets us know when it is in trouble; we don't need to go looking for the problems: the visual workplace makes them stand out like a sore thumb! The logic is fairly simple: we can only solve what we can see, so seeing becomes everything.

There are two types of Visual Management you might encounter at work, or indeed anywhere within your daily life. The first of these is "Visual Display". This is exactly as it sounds. A visual display gives us information. In the workplace, for example, this may include information relating to safety, quality, cost, delivery and, perhaps, a people-related metric. The aim is relatively straightforward: the display is there to give us a snapshot of where we are at this moment in time – or, at least, a moment not too far in the distant past.

To this extent, the properties of a good visual display are clear. Firstly, it needs to be up to date; there is not much worse than approaching a display and finding that none of the data has been updated for a while: on the one hand, it shows that the metrics cannot be that important, and at worst it means that we may have lost control of where we are, or maybe that we don't even care! Secondly, the display must be relevant to the person reading it. If the information displayed means nothing to the audience, they are unlikely to engage with the message, and the board fades into the background, to become another example of corporate wallpaper.

The relevance will also naturally define where the display is situated. General information boards in the workplace tend to be located where there will be the greatest footfall: for instance, inside canteens or at points of entry or exit. Stronger, however, is local information stored at the gemba - the place where the work takes place. Having a Key Performance Indicator (KPI) nearby, which you can actually impact, can be tremendously motivating and empowering.

The second type of Visual Management is "Visual Control". Whereas Visual Display gives us information, Visual Control aims to modify our behaviour. The critical point to a piece of Visual Control is that it should need no interpretation. Take driving a car, for example. Driving is one of the most visually-controlled activities that we carry out, from day to day; most of us are so familiar with it that there will be times when we arrive at work and cannot actually remember our journey there, so ingrained are the Visual Control cues, such as traffic lights, which guided us through the process.

It is surely no accident that we are bombarded with information all day, every day. Much of this data we don't recall absorbing, until we have the strangest urge to buy the product advertised on that billboard we always pass without looking. Business is no different: it sets that top-level goal - the mission statement - then strives to align all activity to it. Often, this mission is focused on the customer and fulfilling that need. Whilst the value-adding workers at the coal face may not recognize how they fit into the more loftier goals held by the organization, the key to success is in the cascade of the measures and behaviours to this level, and in what state they arrive, without diluting the underlying message.

By the time the message of the mission arrives at the shop floor, for example, it may well be in the form of a simple behaviour; a singular, daily action, which makes a small impression on the overall goal.

The parallels with our own efforts to improve are quite revealing. We will all have our top-level ideal or desire, which we are working toward. The question becomes – and, it is no surprise to see this theme emerging again – *"What one, small thing are we going to do today, where we stand, to move toward it?"*

But, the idea that I would like to explore at this juncture is that of visualization. It has long been established, amongst top sportspeople, that visualization can be applied to enhance performance greatly. Indeed, it appears that the brain is unable to distinguish between the reality and the visualization, if the visualization is strong enough. The muscles used in the endeavour of making a putt, for example, fire off as they would under the real stresses and strains of final round competition, even if the action is merely imagined. Dreams are an excellent example of this kind of change in physiology: when we awaken from a nightmare, our body is primed in the "fight or flight response"; we only calm down when we wake and realize that the danger is not real.

We can use visualization as a major part of our efforts. I think we will all have read similar elsewhere: behave as if you have already manifested the focus of your desire.

The logic of the workplace KPI board and company mission can definitely be applied here. We can easily track our progress toward certain goals (perhaps weight loss or saving money toward buying a car). But, care is needed: the data you track should be used as a call to action, rather than a punitive demotivator when targets are occasionally missed. Remember, a missed target is a learning opportunity. Coach yourself. Ask yourself some simple questions: what stopped you achieving your target; what are you going to do differently next time; what is the learning and growth point here?

The most important questions should always be apparent, however: what action are you going to take today, to move that one step toward your definite purpose; how are you going to make that action truly value-adding? As we have already seen, it will be the small, daily actions which add up to your eventual outcome, rather than one, paradigm-shifting event. Of course, these can happen, but we should never be reliant upon that.

Visual Management plays an important part in transparent business, and so it should be in the improvement efforts within our own lives. Transparency is key, because it is this transparency which will speak to our minds on a conscious and subconscious level.

I am sure that this will not be the first book surrounding this subject that you have encountered, so you may already be familiar with visualization, and its applicability to this topic. As we have briefly explored, it is a technique already employed by athletes and sportspeople, the world over. They apply it to gain a few extra percent on the ability that they already have; we, on the other hand, will apply it on a whole different level: to communicate our purpose both to ourselves, on our multiple levels and, through our own neural transmitters, to the Universe itself.

Vision boards are something which many people on this journey before us have used to great effect, so there is no reason why we should not use them, too. The premise is very simple: you display, in one place, pictures of all of the things you would like to draw toward you, and are currently working toward. Perhaps this is your dream home, a luxury sports car, a yacht or a visual representation which somehow encapsulates where you want to be, whatever that looks like to you. Now, it would be fairly easy to stare at a board like this every day and believe that you are communicating something, but the connection to your visualizations should be deeper, and on a more holistic, elemental level. Let us imagine that we are visualizing the manifestation of a new, luxury home. Rather than just look at the picture, visualize yourself walking through the front door. What do each of the rooms look like? What is in them? Perhaps you get the waft of something delicious cooking in the kitchen? You feel excited as you walk around but, most of all, you feel grateful; you feel an overwhelming gratitude for the home and everything in it. You feel it permeating every cell and synapse. You feel thankful that you already have it. Picture yourself sharing the good times with friends and family, encapsulating all of the good that you can do and what you can be. This is the real meaning of the Visual Management system. See it. Feel it. Believe it. Live it.

7

STANDARDIZATION

If you have ever spent time working in pretty much any industry, you will have been told the importance of standardization. However, as with so many of these topics, there are times when standardization is completely misunderstood. First, let us look at standardization from a workplace perspective, then explore what lessons we can draw for our personal work.

In many businesses, standardization is eulogized with something approaching religious zeal. Unfortunately, the true purpose of standardization then becomes unclear, and the benefits become lost. Very often, you can ask the question "What is standardization?" and achieve a response such as: "Standardization is about doing the same thing the same way, each time." This response is not incorrect, per se, but it misses the entire point of the venture.

Often, standardization is embodied within a document. Its name changes, dependent on where you are working but, for the purposes of this discussion, let us call it a "Standard

Operating Procedure", or "SOP", for short. I have often garnered the impression that the Standard Operating Procedure, for many processes, makes its way around the factory, reverently carried on a velvet cushion. It exudes such reverence that it can never be wrong and never be challenged; the very thought of doing so is a heresy, to be discouraged with the utmost vehemence. However, if you think about the work we did when looking at the PDCA Cycle, you will realize that this is a flawed view of standardization.

Standard work should not be the unchallenged endpoint of the process, but merely a springboard from which the next improvement iteration is launched. In the *ACT* phase of the PDCA Cycle, we standardize the improvements that we have made into the amended process - but, remember, it is always our intention to return to the *PLAN* phase and target our next improvement. The PDCA improvement cycle is a never-ending process; the purpose of standardization, during each iteration of this cycle, is to hold and provide the baseline for the next improvement to be made.

Let me illustrate this with a story drawn from a simple home example. Many years ago, my mother had a cookery book. The book bore the outward scars of many an encounter in a busy kitchen: a splash of gravy here, a remnant of pastry there... But, it was when one opened the book that the real story emerged. Over the years, the book had been lent out to various family members - perhaps looking for a recipe for a pie filling or a simple sponge cake - but, when one looked at the recipes and methods within the book, it became clear that there were hundreds of small pencil notations made within its pages: *"Use 200g, not 150g"; "Cook for 25 minutes, not 20"; "Bake at gas mark 5, not gas mark 6";* the book was alive! It was organic! And, what is more, the collective trial and error learning of all of those who had used this resource before was available to me, there and then. I did not have to go through the same culinary trials and tribulations that they did; their skills were now mine.

I think that the parallels with our own desire to iteratively improve our lives are now becoming obvious. Firstly, let us state this again: *if you always do what you always did, you will always get what you always got.* Read that again; it really is that important. Change is not going to beat its way to your door through positive thought alone: you have to take action, and it has to be something different. The life that you have now is the standard which you have set, but that standard is not set in stone - it is merely the jumping-off point for your next improvement. Don't you find that remarkably liberating?

Don't wait to do something tomorrow; don't be put off by the enormity of the task; just do something small today. You will signal your intention with faith in yourself, and send that same electrical signal to the Universe. Momentum and success will surely follow.

Another side to this topic is the conventional thinking that we bring into our efforts. The very fact that you are interested in a book of this nature most probably illustrates that, on a superficial level, at least, you wish to challenge the thinking with which you have lived. But, at this stage, we must take a moment to reflect: challenging our own thinking is going to be incredibly hard, and this is where a great deal of work may well lie. The enemy here may be deeply ingrained beliefs, which we have inherited and absorbed over time, without realizing it.

Imagine, for example, that as you grew up, money was tight - this should not be too difficult for many of us. Within that sort of environment, it is easy to pick up the belief that you shouldn't have money - that it would somehow make you a traitor to your background. Worse, you may subconsciously feel that money is inherently evil, and that it can only be accrued in abundance by those who have done something immoral or wrong. In this case, no matter what you wish for on a conscious level, it is probable that your subconscious mind is not aligned with this thinking. So, how should we challenge that standardized mindset? Perhaps, during our visualizations, we might see ourselves performing a service with our newfound wealth? Monetary wealth undoubtedly gives us all the opportunity to help those less fortunate than ourselves. Furthermore, through this very act of sharing our abundance we, through the law of increasing returns, can create further abundance, so that we can share even more. When you give, feel good about it, and soon your subconscious will pick up on the idea that money can be used for good. Everything should then be aligned.

To introduce our next topic of discussion, let us return to the example of the cookbook. If you remember, our book was a wonderful compendium of collective knowledge: in baking a simple sponge cake, I had available to me, through the numerous pencil notations, not only the knowledge of the author of the recipe, but also the collective know-how of everyone who had made that cake before me. In my mind, this raises two essential and closely-related points, which we shall now review in turn.

The first of these discussion points, named by those who

have trodden this path, is the *"mastermind alliance"*. In basic terms, this is the practice of drawing those people toward you who are already successful, most usefully in the field of your chosen activity.

This is where we have a profound advantage over the many who have gone before. In these days of the internet and social media, it is amazingly easy to gain access to many of the finest minds, in pretty much any field of effort. In the world of personal improvement alone, it is possible to landscape your media feeds so that you are being fed and immersed by positive information and suggestion, on an almost minute-by-minute basis. Naturally, care should be taken to filter out the negative elements from your social media, but it is entirely possible to create a bespoke account, which is simply full of the thoughts of wonderful people. What is more, you can gain direct access to people you admire and be privy to their thoughts and ideas. This is a tremendous opportunity: you can create powerful groups at the touch of only a few buttons. No previous generation has had this sort of gift.

That all said, there is naturally no substitute for meeting and learning from people in real life. There will still be negative people within your world, for certain, but you now have the opportunity to help them. Go to work on them; be to them the inspiration that your mastermind group is to you.

I think it is tremendously inspiring to think that positive people across the world are becoming connected via the internet. But, the truth is even starker: we were already connected. The whole planet is made up of the same building blocks, with particles vibrating at different rates.

This, in essence, is the entire explanation of the Law of Attraction: like particles and forces attract one another. So, our task is simple: we must raise our vibration, so that it meets the frequency of the elements of life which we wish to attract. "Frequency" is an interesting word here. Back in the good old days of analogue radio, you had to be very precise in your tuning, to get perfect reception for your radio station of choice. Sometimes you could tune between two different stations and get a strange mix of both. The parallels are clear; keep your radio tuned to the right station.

In this day and age, the most successful and well-known businesses operate from within the community. They are no longer faceless sentinels, where the townsfolk troop off to work as part of a smoky, clanking machine, only to all troop home again, upon the sounding of a giant, steam-bellowing horn, unable to speak about what they have done. But, companies cannot afford to sit outside of the community now; they need to embrace it, nurture it and, to a certain extent, lead it. It has taken industry a long, long time to realize this, but people really are the greatest asset and lifeblood of all businesses. What is a company, after all, but a collection of people, working toward a shared goal? Take those people away, and what is left? So, it follows that when businesses are successful within a community, they have a responsibility to look after not only their workers, but also their families and the larger community, itself. Part of this will be by employing their collective experience and reach, by funding projects within the locality. Initiatives like this go a long way to adding shareholder value and creating brand and employee loyalty. Through sponsoring students in their studies, these businesses can also assure their future in quickly identifying and capturing the talent which will eventually take everyone - the business and the community – onward, into the future.

Once again, the parallels are hugely apparent with our own efforts to continually improve our lives. The sharing of abundance, in whatever form that manifests, is vitally important in creating more abundance, which will enable you to share even more. Some of you reading this book will be running or looking to run businesses. You will have a tremendous opportunity to demonstrate the power of the community-minded company. The big corporations, whatever you may think of them, are wonderfully placed to demonstrate the power of giving and sharing, perhaps even more so than the governments of this world. We can all be a part of that. If you are lucky enough to attract an abundance of money into your life, give a little away - it will help you feel good about money, and you will undoubtedly attract more. Be the hero in your family, street or town - you will inspire others through your actions, and the snowball will grow; you will make a difference many times greater than your original reach.

8

COACHING - THE GROW MODEL

There are many obstacles to overcome in the improvement of our lives. After all, if it were that easy, there would be no sense of worth in achieving anything.

Some of the resistance to our work will no doubt come from family and friends. Of course, we would like to think that they would only want the best for us, but seeing somebody step out and take a change of direction can be a challenge for those around us; some might even subconsciously try to sabotage us, without even realizing it. For those who are not familiar with the concepts of this and many other books, the initial reaction to opportunity will be negative and fear based. Indeed, this is one of the major barriers to overcome, and one I still struggle with to this day: namely, the remaining drive to make decisions based on fear rather than positivity, and a sense of trusting adventure.

Similar reticence exists in the workplace. At work,

decisions are often made through opinion. Further choices are often based on the opinion of the group or person who was able to make their case loudest, or most aggressively - the rest of the business follows behind, timidly. One of the early challenges, in any business, is to get it to shift to an accurate, data-based process, making decisions based on *"I know"*, rather than *"I think"*. Remember that those around you, including yourself, will have been taught to think in a certain way - it may even be so ingrained that merely aiming for success is frowned upon. Often, it is seen as something of a betrayal of one's roots and surroundings.

What I am essentially saying here is that the biggest obstacle to your own success is the ingrained thoughts and mores that you yourself bring to the table. You may not even know that they exist, such is the depth of this challenge.

During my recovery from gambling addiction, I was introduced to the twelve-step programme. If you are interested, by all means look this up; there are some interesting elements there. One of the early steps recommended was to take an unblinking personal inventory of oneself. I have to admit that this was a step I did not wholly adhere to; I discussed what I had done, during my shares with the group, but it was almost exclusively a surface-level picture. The personal-level thinking I did was limited and wholly negative in approach. In truth, I was frightened by what I might see.

The Japanese have incorporated this personal inventory into the Kaizen model. They call it "Hansei" - in other words, creating a learning organization through self-reflection. They strongly recognize the need, within each PDCA improvement cycle, to take a step back and reflect upon the learning they can draw from the activities which have taken place. They can then apply a *5S* logic in sorting this feedback: what do they need to keep and be aware of for next time, and what can be safely jettisoned as chaff?

One of the key points that you will be starting to ascribe to Kaizen is the need for structure. Structure promotes repeatability and reproducibility, when the model is applied with faith and honesty. So now, in order to help us to reflect with structure, we will discuss the *GROW* model.

GROW is another four-stage model, which is used in interpersonal coaching. If you can find somebody who you wholly trust, who is proficient in the model, then you are lucky indeed - add them to your mastermind group immediately! However, I am comfortable that this can also be used effectively for self-reflection.

There are a couple of reasons for this thinking. Firstly,

the success of this approach relies upon the honesty of the coachee. If you are unable to be honest with yourself, then this is your first battle. What are the causes of this? If you have not taken this personal inventory, you are likely to struggle with any approach toward improving your life, and well may be subconsciously sabotaging your own efforts. If you are happy to approach this method with unblinking honesty, I think you will be rewarded.

This links to the second reason. A coach who applies the *GROW* model does not have to be all-seeing and worldly-wise; the trick (not that it *is* a trick) is in the carefully constructed questions the coach asks. The answers, in the main, already exist inside the person receiving the coaching. Sometimes, the response is merely a commitment to go out and find the answer. As with all of our Kaizen thinking, a commitment to an action plan, however simple or complex, is what we are seeking to achieve.

So, let us now look at the four stages of the *GROW* model in turn, and think about some useful questions to ask.

G is for "GOAL":

What is your goal?
How will you feel when you have reached it?

How will you know when you have reached it?

What does success look like?

Why is this something that you want to do?

R is for "REALITY":

What is your current position?

Do you have the skills to reach your goal?

When have you tried this before, what went well?

When you have tried this before, what was challenging?

How will your support network encourage you to reach your target?

O is for "OPTIONS":

How many different ways are there to reach your goal? Can you list them?

Does your goal have to be reached in a certain way?

What would you do if you don't know the answer?

What are your short-term goals?

What alternatives are there to your plan?

What would the journey look like if everything went perfectly?

W is for "WILL":

What are you willing to do to reach your goal?

What are you going to commit to doing today?

What is your target for the end of next week?

As you can see, if you can go through these questions with someone close, then I believe that you will gain tremendous value. Even if you have to ask yourself these questions, the outcomes required are that you can raise awareness of your current situation and the pathways available, to get to where you want to go. In addition, it is about taking responsibility for your journey. It is sometimes easy to blame outside factors for making this journey difficult, but what is the reality? It is more likely that, at that moment, we are being governed by fear.

Be honest with yourself. I used to think that I wanted to be hugely wealthy, but when I thought about it, I realized that I don't need millions in the bank. Nowadays, my definition of wealthy is owning a good-sized home and having the ability to work for myself, as a writer. It is about a healthy mind and body, supported by my flexible working day, successful relationships around me, and the chance to help others, whether that be sharing with friends and family, or those less fortunate than myself. I used to think that I would like to win the lottery and gain that fairytale pot of millions but, strangely, the more I think about it, the more that idea does not feel right. I want to have earnt the money, through my own hard work and application - only then would it truly mean something.

One of the critical fundamentals of the Toyota Production System is long-term thinking. This is always something which I have personally found extremely difficult to apply, both in the business environment and in terms of personal improvement. Within business, everything is set up to create a backdrop where long-term thinking is wholly discouraged. Let us think about a typical career path: the aim, in general terms, is to rise through the ranks, as quickly as possible. With this mindset, the career-oriented individual always has half an eye on the next job they are going for. This creates an environment which prioritizes quick wins, regardless of whether or not these initiatives have long-term potential. By the time a particular solution is discovered not to be effective, the individual responsible has often moved on, and the next influencer has moved in, who then naturally wants to put their own individual stamp on the department or area. Eventually, we have a series of flavour-of-the-month scenarios, wherein weary workers claim to have "seen this all before", as one manager overhauls the work of their predecessor. The upshot is a confusion of short-term decision making, with no alignment to a greater strategy.

This might sound a little counterintuitive, as many aspects of lean certainly can: for much of our discussions, we have been emphasizing small daily actions - activities which can lead to quick wins - but now I am encouraging you to think in the longer term. The key, of course, is to link the two together: look toward the big plan, but go after it in bite-size pieces; you can never become a millionaire without making your first dollar.

The other benefit of long-term thinking is that temporary setbacks are just that: temporary. At the moment, I am trying to find an agent for a novel which I have written. However, at the time of writing, I think I am at about twelve rejections. In the short term, this feels like a disaster; if my goal were to publish that particular book, it would be a struggle. However, I recognize that my goal is not specifically to publish that book but, more accurately, to become a writer in general - that is one of the reasons why I am now working on this book. In terms of my novel, I may soon have to face the fact that it is not currently good enough. And, here is where my long-term goal kicks in: I still aim to be a writer, but my long-term thinking means that my purpose is still alive and kicking. Essentially, if I want to carry on pursuing this purpose, I have two choices: I can either rewrite the novel or, if it really is that bad, to abandon that particular work and try with something else. The key here is that my long-term thinking is the enabler, to drive me through the short-term pain. In actual fact, the novel in question is my fourth attempt - the first two attempts are, sadly, lost, though the first was almost certainly irredeemable. Both, however, were valuable points on my learning journey. The long-term goal remains intact, but I am now wiser and more experienced.

I can draw a similar experience from my previous gambling days. In the long term, my goal was to give up gambling forever - but, when emerging from an addiction, forever seems like a very long time. Often, the advice given was to give up *"just for today"* - or even smaller time frames, if that felt intolerable. However, the long-term objective was always the motivating factor. Perhaps this was even just the notion of being able to look oneself in the mirror again but, regardless, there was always something to aim for.

The same is true in the business environment. Continuous Improvement is a journey, not a destination; you will never reach perfection, but you will get closer and closer and closer. The ideal state of a business may be defined by an "Ideal State Value Stream Map", but the gap will be bridged by a number of "Future State Maps", in increasing degrees of development. However, without the Ideal State - which could be five to ten years away - there can never be a collective and focused vision to work toward.

Another concept to draw back into this discussion is, once more, that of Hansei. Hansei is a Japanese term which corresponds with reflection - we discussed it briefly when thinking about the *CHECK* phase of the PDCA Cycle, and again when approaching the *GROW* model. Hansei is a wonderful concept. Imagine that you have spent hours walking through noisy cityscapes, only to then arrive in the countryside. Can you imagine drawing in that fresh, country air through your nostrils, then giving a big sigh, as you exhale the last of the city from your lungs? Imagine lying on the side of sunlit hill, feeling the warmth, as you look back into the valley, where the city lies. This is Hansei: every so often, you have to stop, look at the work that you have done and evaluate it. And yes, at this point, remind yourself how far you have come.

I have been present at meetings where the detail of the day has made it difficult to focus on the positive progress made over time. When that second fact has been pointed out, the work of the ongoing daily actions comes much more sharply into focus, and momentum is renewed. This is why remembering or documenting your starting point is so important.

We can also tie that starting point back to your next target, whether that is an important milestone or the realization of your entire purpose. Remember, Hansei should be a positive experience of growth. Even if you are reflecting on temporary failure, remember that it is only that: temporary.

One of the most rewarding elements of this reflection can also occur when the going seems at its most challenging. It is the chance to look back and see how far away - down in the distant valley - your starting point is. Take a deep breath inward, turn back to face the front, and press on toward that peak. You are going in the right direction, and you have already come so far.

9

TPM

Now, let us have a review, whilst at the same time introducing a new topic.

"Total Productive Maintenance" has been around, in various guises, for many decades. Some say it was introduced by a Toyota supplier in the 1950s; others point to American industry at the turn of the 20th century. Wherever it came from, the important thing to note is how it encapsulates a total approach, similarly to the Kaizen enterprise.

TPM (we will dispense with the full title from here on in) is designed to maximize the output of a working environment (typically a factory), through caring for its machines, processes and people. This is achieved through delivery and adherence to the "eight pillars" of TPM, with the primary focus falling on the equipment the organization uses to be productive. Let us introduce the pillars here, then look at each in turn. Before we do, however - as if we were building a house - we need to construct some firm foundations upon which to erect our eight pillars.

If I promised you a recap, this is where it starts: learning through repetition, application and embedment, we will progress together. The foundation of TPM is a topic with which we engaged right back at the beginning of this book: namely, *5S*. Even with the simple understanding we currently have of TPM, doing preparatory *5S* makes sense. Using *SORT*, we remove the clutter from the workplace, leaving the equipment we actually need. *SET* places the equipment where it is needed, and also manages any consumables and parts required by the machines. *SHINE* begins to clean the equipment, in order that we can inspect it: are there any broken dials or displays; do all of the emergency stops function; are there any lubricant leaks visible, after cleaning? *STANDARDIZE* will tell us what the optimum machine setup looks like, and *SUSTAIN* will bring this all together, in a spirit of harmony and ongoing improvement. We are now ready for our pillars.

AUTONOMOUS MAINTENANCE

We previously discussed this concept by thinking about ownership of a car: when cleaning our car, we are simultaneously inspecting it. From this starting point, we can begin to accept some of the simpler maintenance tasks, such as checking the tyre pressures or oil and water levels. The same is true in the workplace: the operators of a machine become its owners, developing within the business by learning new Autonomous Maintenance skills. This leaves the actual maintenance department free to fulfil their primary requirements and hedge the risk inherent in the bigger potential breakdowns.

We have also spoken about how the step of Autonomous Maintenance applies to our own work on ourselves. The human body and the human brain are two of the most complex and marvellous machines in existence, anywhere in the Universe. You are truly unique. Your brain will conceive the path, and your body will take you on it.

PLANNED MAINTENANCE

Planned Maintenance is exactly what it says it is: the planned maintenance of the machines which underpin the successful manufacturing enterprise. Typically, this will be done during a shutdown period, like the summer holidays, to allow for the key equipment to be stripped down and thoroughly checked over. The difficulty can come when you switch the machines back on for the first time: some equipment will be so used to running continuously, it will not take kindly to having been switched off; much of the initial material may now be scrap, as the machine naturally settles into the tolerances, once more.

There is so much here which offers parallels to the work we are undertaking. Firstly, allowing ourselves planned downtime becomes vitally important. We work to live; once we begin to live to work, it could be argued that we have crossed a line (however, it must be pointed out that there are those of us out there who live like sharks: they simply cannot stop swimming). Perhaps the key is to find the balance which works for us, and the recuperative value of a holiday can never be underestimated!

But, this is where the apparent contradictions continue: we noted above that machines do not work bang up to speed and quality when they are first switched on, and the same is true of the human-machine. So, if you are planning to go on holiday for a week, perhaps your overall schedule should allow for two weeks, to allow you to slowly ramp up your activity upon return. The most important thing, however, is to get going again.

I had started a gym schedule a little while back, and had

a European business trip on the horizon. I used this week-long trip as the excuse not to go to the gym for the whole week before it, because "it just wasn't worth it". I did not go to the gym again for many months afterward. Sportspeople - particularly those who pit their skill directly against others - speak of a difference between "fitness" and "match fitness". For footballers, match fitness might not actually come for six to eight weeks into a season, although they are generally very fit all year round.

In terms of our Planned Maintenance, the maintenance teams then have the ability, throughout the year, to collect data relating to the machines - such data may include *"Mean Time to Repair"* (MTTR) or *"Mean Time to Failure"* (MTTF). The understanding of such data can be fundamental - when it comes to ordering spares, for example. Whilst we would never want to be caught without a spare on the shelf, we similarly would not want to hold many years' worth of stock - this would be accruing the waste of inventory. Also, whilst we would never plan for failure, if you know roughly when your machine might fail, you can plan to have your important jobs carried out prior to that danger time.

QUALITY MAINTENANCE

As I type this book, any words I misspell are underlined in red by the word-processing programme - this can be seen as an element of "Quality Maintenance". This topic seeks to build error detection and prevention into the manufacturing process, to help pursue the aspiration of zero defects. Where errors occur, it encourages Root-Cause Analysis, and could be followed up with such tools as "Statistical Process Control" (SPC) and *"Poka-Yoke"* (mistake-proofing). Of these subjects, I think Root-Cause Analysis deserves its own section, so we will return to this later.

How might we apply the pillar of Quality Maintenance to our own Continuous Improvement efforts? I think this comes back to the idea of error detection. We have already discussed how the human-machine is one of the most remarkable creations around; its complexity and properties of healing and self-renewal are, quite simply, astounding. It is the ultimate transportation system for the human brain. But, if the body is stunning and complex, this is nothing when compared to the brain. As humans, we have reached into the depths of space, but we still cannot comprehend the full workings of the brain. What we can do is respect this mind-body connection and observe it, quietly: it will tell us when we need to correct a potential problem. Whether this be by a hunch, or the feelings which arrive with the onset of a cold, the mind-body will give us early warning signals, which can enable us to offset with some greater call to action. Sometimes, it may even be that voice in your head, telling you to do something; to go after that opportunity. Listen to it; listen to your mind and your machine: it is seldom wrong.

FOCUSED IMPROVEMENT

This is what this whole book is about, so let us take the opportunity to call back in on our collective goal: it is our goal to apply the Continuous Improvement methodologies - which have been successful all over the world, across multiple businesses, in all kinds of sector - to our own lives. Wherever we stand, whatever our circumstances, we are resolved to apply daily, focused actions toward a target or plan, in which we are wholly engaged and believe in, with every fibre of our being.

Sounds easy, doesn't it? Well, the truth is that it isn't. That is why not everyone on the planet is doing it! Not everyone is cut out to follow this decisive course of action. *You* are. The very fact that you are reading this book demonstrates that, beyond all doubt. Congratulate yourself, but not too much: you've got actions to be getting on with!

EARLY EQUIPMENT MANAGEMENT

You are the owner of a factory, and you have just shelled out on a new, super-duper, spangly, sparkly machine. Early Equipment Management is now what you need to be doing, right from the off, before the machine has even been craned off of the truck.

By understanding the design, usability, reliability and quality issues around the design of new equipment and products, you can take off vertically, and meet your targets head-on.

For me, the way I would relate this to our own efforts is to describe how we would conduct the learning, the self-inventory and the research, before diving headlong into a project. Proper planning can go a long way to ensuring success.

However, a word of caution: don't let planning override everything else. What do I mean by this? If we take my example of writing a novel again: the temptation is to keep going back to the manuscript, tweaking a word here, altering a phrase there, rereading, restyling and redoing. In my mind, I convince myself that I am moving forward, creating something which is ever nearer to being released into the world. In truth, I am putting this moment off, by telling myself, again and again, that I am not ready. With proper planning, research and scheduling at the front end, you can give yourself the timeline to complete your project. Stick to the dates, and there will be less temptation to apply the brakes.

TRAINING AND EDUCATION

When a new piece of equipment arrives in a business, it is often not as simple as switching it on and starting to use it. Firstly, the staff whose job it is to use it will probably need training in its operation and routine maintenance processes (see Autonomous Maintenance). Secondly, the maintenance team will need to be trained in the higher level and more complex maintenance tasks and strategies, which they will need to employ to ensure that installation and ongoing usage performs effectively in the future. But, the need for training and education may well be much, much greater than that; the whole enterprise needs to be aligned with this thinking.

This is where we must recall that Total Productive Maintenance is not merely a strategy employed by those who look after the machines and those who operate them - far from it. It is a business-wide initiative, which seeks to orientate the whole workforce to one outlook: namely, that of customer-focused Continuous Improvement, or Kaizen. This is a tough job: introducing the Kaizen skillset into a business might take a year; changing the mindset and values could take five or six years - perhaps even longer. Worse still, if some employees, in key lower- or middle-management positions, are not, at best, willing to align with your efforts, or are, at worst, actively blocking them, you may need to manage them out of your business.

We have already covered most of this ground in some of our earlier discussions. We may have people and thought processes within our life who are holding us back, whether unintentionally or even actively. This is almost certain to be true when considering our own minds, and the beliefs that our journey to this point has given us. We must be unblinking in uncovering these improvement opportunities, and doing the preparatory work required to fix them at their root cause.

It may also be that, on a more practical level, we will need to learn some new skills - that may be learning how a website works, learning the best exercises to use, or maybe a new language. But, whatever we do, from formal learning to informal self-examination, we must ensure that this effort is aligned to our overall plan, and adding value to it.

SAFETY, HEALTH AND ENVIRONMENT

One of the commonly targeted outcomes of any TPM effort is that of zero accidents. This can relate both to the use of machines and to the workplace in general. There is ample legislation here in the U.K. to manage "Safety, Health and Environment" within the workplace, which all fall under the *Health and Safety at Work Act* of 1974. Safety is now rightly the number one priority within every workplace across the developed world, and it is underpinned by the application of risk assessment, within the workplace.

Risk assessment can be done in a number of different ways, but my preference is for the scored matrix - that is just the way I think: I like to see things quantitively; you may well be different. In a quantitative risk assessment, two elements are measured and rated, on a scale of 1-10. The elements under review are normally *Severity* (S), multiplied by *Likelihood* (L); the returned value is referred to as the "Risk Rating" (RR) - as you can see, the highest risk rating is 100. This would be the nightmare scenario: i.e. an event was almost certain to occur, and when it did, it would cause long-term disability or even death. You can then identify what countermeasures are already in place and measure the remaining risk, using the same system: this is your "Residual Risk Rating". At this point, you can ask yourself whether you have done enough to mitigate the risk within the process.

During the early days of my recovery from gambling addiction, I was frequently undertaking "dynamic" risk assessments. A dynamic risk assessment is less formal; it is an assessment which you make on the move. When you cross the road, you essentially run through a dynamic risk assessment: *Is that car far enough away; how fast is it moving?* In recovery from gambling, these questions might be replaced by: *am I carrying any money; do I have access to a newspaper; is there anything happening today which might trigger the gambling behaviour?* For a couple of years, I was held accountable for every penny in my bank account; I didn't read the racing pages in the paper; I turned off the television, if horseracing was on; I cancelled all of my gambling accounts; I removed everything which posed a risk.

So, again, coming back to our Continuous Improvement efforts, what can we identify as posing a risk to our elevation? Our own self-doubts and belief systems? The well-meaning cynicism and limiting beliefs of others? The perception that we don't have the skill or the time? Our ability to become distracted by the chatter of the daily world? Even simple countermeasures can help: something as simple as, when settling down to a task, to further your intention, put on your work shoes. This can work wonders; your slippers automatically slip you into a different frame of mind! When I sit down to write, I like to place the television remote controls out of reach: that way, I have to make an effort to break my activity to fetch them.

To go back to our machines for a moment, the first thing that needs to happen before maintenance is that the machine should be safely shut down and isolated from its power supply. There have been numerous horror stories in which machines have been switched back on, whilst maintenance workers were still inside. One method to ensure this does not happen is safety lock-offs: in this situation, the power supply switch is inside a small cabinet, which the maintenance engineer will padlock shut, whilst he or she carries out their work. Similarly, all machines are routinely fitted with emergency stops, which shut down the machine immediately when activated - these might be the big, round buttons which are remarkably tempting to push or, better still, light-beams or pressure-mats, which are triggered by either being broken or registering weight.

I think that from our personal perspectives, at least, we need to recognize our personal risk factors and not be frightened of pushing our own personal emergency stops when the direst circumstances arise. However – and, you will find that lean and Continuous Improvement is often counterintuitive - more often than not, we need to push straight through these perceived risks, because they are not rational risk assessments; most of the time they are fear-based emotions, with a root cause somewhere. Self-discovery and evaluation might be scary, but it seldom hurts anyone. Here, it will free us to achieve.

TPM IN ADMINISTRATION

For many years, the factory floor has come under the scrutiny of scores of experts, all looking to improve the piece of the business which everyone sees: the gemba; the place where the actual product is put together. This makes a certain degree of sense, since this is where the money is made, and is the point nearest to the customer. But, whilst that effort took place, the offices went along in their own happy way, creating just as much waste, bloated processes and in-trays of work, which invisibly impacted the capability and effectiveness of the business. Well, I say "invisibly", but often this wasn't the case.

Let's say that someone forgot to order a part. The pain of that missed transaction would not be felt at the point of order – in purchasing, say - it would be felt at the point of fit, in the gemba itself. The replacement part might be expedited in, at extra expense, and the product experiencing the shortage would eventually come back into the line, being marked as a negative on the "Delivery Schedule Achievement" metric. The product would eventually ship (costing the business more), and the opportunity to learn about the trigger point in the purchasing chain would be lost.

This is what drove and continues to drive TPM in administration: namely, the realization that there were untapped improvement opportunities within the transactional areas of lean business enterprises. The support processes are just as vital to the overall goal as the assembly or production processes.

In wholly transactional businesses, this is even more pivotal. We all want our utility bills calculated correctly, or our insurance claim dealt with swiftly and efficiently. I have trained lean in all sorts of different sectors, including some which didn't even realize that they needed it - the point being that lean is for everyone, and everyone can gain something out of personal improvement. No matter what your goal, you can start to work toward it today, and these techniques are applicable and available to you. Be thankful for your starting point and springboard from there. Adopt and adapt; find what works for you. Experiment, but stick to the principles. The pathways are all here.

We will close our discussion on TPM by briefly exploring one of its principle measures of success: TPM exists to bolster a metric known as "Overall Equipment Effectiveness", or OEE. It is a useful measure, which gives us a figure roughly quantifying how well we are utilizing the equipment we have in the workplace. I will not go into the full calculation here but, needless to say, the final figure is derived from the product of three inputs: these are *availability* (e.g. uptime and downtime), *performance* (short stops; slow running, etc.) and *quality* (percentage right first time). Remember, this is a yield style calculation: if you were scoring 90% in each of availability, performance and quality, your overall OEE figure would be just under 73% - hardly impressive! What becomes key is understanding where you are losing that longed-for effectiveness.

The experts in this field talk about the six big losses - the six major reasons which erode "Overall Equipment Effectiveness". In essence, there are many reasons gathered under the banner of the six, but I think that, for our purposes, we can look at the main topic headings for now. The six big losses are:

BREAKDOWNS;
SET-UP AND ADJUSTMENTS;
REDUCED SPEED;
PRODUCTION REJECTS;
START-UP REJECTS;
SMALL STOPS.

As you can see, each of these losses will impact on one of the three elements of our Overall Equipment Effectiveness calculation (OEE), which we now know to be a product of three contributory measures: *availability x performance x quality.*

Let us now look at each of these losses in turn, with all that we have learnt in mind, and explore further how they might be applicable.

BREAKDOWNS

Breakdowns often means equipment failure; something has broken. Perhaps it is something you are working on, which just hasn't done what you had hoped. At that point of realization, your own personal response is absolutely crucial: are you going to become disheartened and give up? Because, let me tell you, this is by far the easiest course of action.

Maybe, every so often, you need a rest for a day or two. Part of avoiding the breakdowns in your efforts will be to understand the triggers which have derailed you in the past. We come back to our *GROW* model coaching questions again: when you tried this before, what went well; when you did this in the past, what stopped your progress?

SET-UP AND ADJUSTMENTS

In the old days, particularly with diesel cars, you needed to treat them gently when they first started running, especially on those cold, dark, winter mornings. The same is true of some machines: they need to be coaxed to full speed, lovingly warmed up to achieve their optimum output. This difference can be thought of as one aspect of *set-up and adjustment* losses.

When writing, for me, getting going is the difficult bit. It is the same as exercise: the thought of going to the gym can be a little daunting but, once there, you knuckle down and put in a good session. Similarly, when changing from one activity to another, this is a danger point, at which you may lose momentum.

The same is true of machines: in the past, it may have taken a huge amount of work to change the setting on a machine, to run one product over the one which had just finished. The solution to avoid this set-up time used to be simple: keep running the first product on a bigger batch, to get our money's worth. But, this only produced waste. Can you remember which one? That's right: *overproduction*, which in turn duplicates every waste in the process.

What is more, in the case of product, there was the possibility of creating a push system and having an excess of inventory which the market simply did not want. This set of circumstances created a whole field of study within lean manufacturing, namely that of set-up reduction, or "Single Minute Exchange of Dies" (SMED). The logic is simple: the quicker I can set up my machine, the longer I can run it. Also, is there anything which can be prepped whilst the machine is still running, rather than doing it while the machine is down? From experience, I know that I am most likely to lose momentum when swapping from one task to another, but I am not good at sticking to one task for a long time, either. This is where I have to apply extra vigilance and fall back onto my simple reward system. Also, can I draw activities into parallel, or place them at more advantageous times? For example, in periods when I have tried meditation, I like to do this before bed, so that I am already relaxed and can slip into sleep easier. If I am listening to a podcast or some other audio material, it makes sense to parallelize that activity with something else, like ironing, so that I can maximize the use of my time. Of course, this won't be appropriate in all cases, but it is definitely something worth thinking about.

REDUCED SPEED

This can be an interesting one, in a number of ways. In some cases, the running speed on a machine will be reduced when we just don't trust it in some way. Perhaps we are concerned that we may start to produce defects, or maybe we haven't done any maintenance in a while, and are worried that full speed might induce a breakdown.

Sometimes, however, it is the good old human factor; for some reason, people like twisting dials. Even better if they can time the production run to come to an end just at the end of their shift, so that the difficult set-up can be left to the workers who are just coming on! Again, the key here is to gather the awareness of what is causing these reductions in speed.

It is very similar to the set-up topic from our own personal perspective. It might be becoming clear by now that the work is all about realigning yourself, so that you will interact with the world at a higher and more productive frequency. Yes, the work is about attaining that frequency, but the majority of the effort will be in maintaining it.

We will all have times when we are sad or down - that is life. What counts is our reaction. My beloved grandmother passed away during the course of my writing this book. I didn't do much writing during that time but, even as I delivered her eulogy, I knew some good had to come from those circumstances. We, her family, were there to celebrate, rather than mourn. My work in the immediate future would be dedicated to her and driven by her memory. The main thing was that I permitted myself to run at a slower speed, for a while. You have that permission, too: recognize what might cause you to lose focus and take some time out to address it. True, we are all looking to improve our external world, but that is a reflection of what is within. Our real work begins there, with ourselves.

PRODUCTION REJECTS

In manufacturing, the main focus tends to be on reducing defects in production. On occasion, this may not be the right focus - at least, not entirely - but the output (e.g. defective parts or product) is the most obvious manifestation of difficulties and challenges within the business - even more so if these defects reach our eternal customer.

You would think that machines would not produce defects, considering that they are the ultimate expression of reproducibility and repeatability. The old saying goes that *"people are not machines"*, but then, by this analogy, machines are not machines, either. Given time, their capability will drift, and their outputs will subtly change.

The answer to this is "Statistical Process Control" (SPC), which we mentioned earlier. The concept is relatively simple, but the outcome, like many simple ideas, is compelling. In essence, most machined parts are not made to a single, specific measure, but rather fall within a tolerance. Let us imagine that we are manufacturing pins: there will be a maximum acceptable thickness defined for the part; likewise, there will also be a minimum acceptable thickness - these are the parameters of our process, or the "Upper and Lower Control Limits" (UCL and LCL). As long as our machine is producing pins whose diameter falls between the UCL and LCL, we are happy; anything outside of these tolerances is a defect. This is where SPC comes in: as part of the machine process, we can set the machine to measure the diameter of its own product, which can be fed to a computer display. In an ideal world, the production values will be at the midpoint of the UCL and LCL; these would be near-perfect pins. But, over time, the display may show that the thickness is creeping slowly toward one of the two tolerances. This is the beauty of Statistical Process Control: I can set rules for human intervention, which means that I can make adjustments to the machine before we start to produce defective parts. I have the ability to be proactive in understanding that I may be about to go off-track, before it happens.

I don't think that we need to look too far for the parallels to our own lives. Perhaps we haven't fully dealt with some negativity or bad mood, and know that we are about to go into a situation where we are likely to pick an argument. Perhaps we are going into a meeting, knowing that we are unprepared. Wouldn't it be better to speak with that loved one after you have calmed down, or cancel your attendance at the meeting? Things will go wrong, but not everything has to be inevitable. Nothing happens instantly in this life; there are always warning signs. If we learn to recognize what triggers our negative responses - the special cause variation within our moods - we can address that. and be truly self-determining.

START-UP REJECTS

Sometimes, there is nothing more disruptive that you can do to a machine than switch it off. Factory shutdown periods are a case in point.

Perhaps it is summertime, and everyone is going on holiday for two weeks. This is the primary time for the maintenance department to go around and do their scheduled work on the machines. This they do. Then, the workers come back and switch on the machines, and this is where the fun begins: everything is now out of spec. Defects start to accrue, and the operating team find themselves scratching their heads, twisting knobs and tapping dials, trying to get their machines to run the way that they used to. This is one example of the cause of *"start-up rejects"*. Sometimes, the option is taken to run slower for this first period, while the machine settles back into nominal production.

Starting slow, whilst we get used to something, has been something of a theme for us, too. Remember all those unused gym memberships, sitting in drawers from February onward? Remember all those times you have tried to change your life before, but it just didn't work out? Looking at it from a slightly different perspective, I think it was the writer Sidonie-Gabrielle Colette who, upon sitting down each morning to write, would throw away the last sheet she had completed the night before. This rigour meant that the final words, which had been produced when fatigued, were always replaced afresh, once she started her "machine" again, the following day.

SMALL STOPS

On those occasions in the past, when I have had the opportunity to work at home, I approached it with mixed feelings. True, it would save a couple of hours sitting in traffic - a pastime which I have never enjoyed. True, it may also mean that I could linger in bed, a little longer than usual. But, deep down, I knew that there were threats to my productivity. These came from the "small stops". Whether it was making myself a cup of tea, or telling myself that I would just put the washing on, or grab a sandwich - whatever it was - my flow was always blocked by these distractions. Similarly, as I am writing this, I have just been reading up on Colette! It was never my intention to do so. In machines, this could be clearing a jam, for example. It is those little distractions which eat the time and reduce the flow.

These are the things we need to approach with vigilance. Maybe it is even catching those thoughts which come to our mind - those which have the ability to undermine our intentions. The more we do so, the stronger and more elongated our positive thinking will become until, one day, it becomes our frequency raising norm.

10

ANALYSIS TOOLS

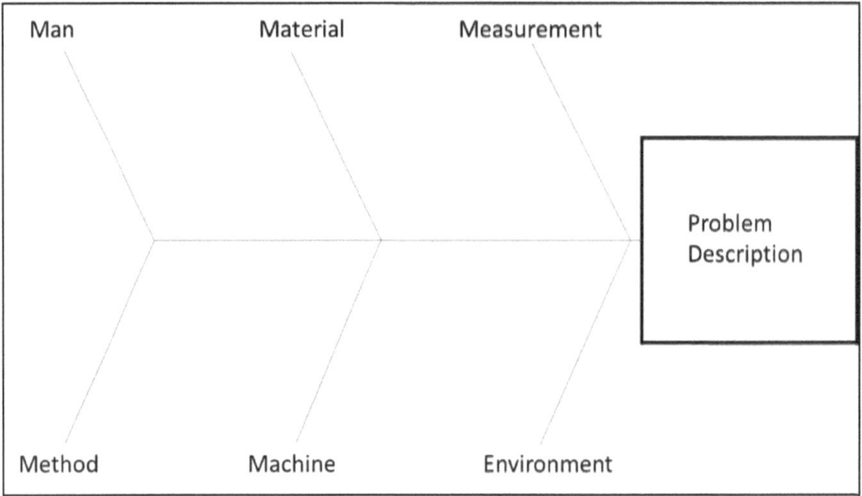

The diagram above will be familiar to anyone who has done any problem solving in a work environment. It is known by many different names, including, for obvious reasons, the "fishbone diagram". Other names include the "cause and effect diagram" and, for the Japanese fans out there, the "Ishikawa diagram", after the initiator Kaoru Ishikawa, Professor of Engineering at the University of Tokyo.

So, what is the Ishikawa diagram? Essentially, it is a visual tool which provides us with a framework to bring together all of our thinking about one problem, in the same place. To begin, we write our problem in the head of the fish, then all the possible causes of the problem, however likely or unlikely, are written onto the spines.

Within the workplace, this is best achieved within a group brainstorming environment. Now, good brainstorming itself is something of an art form: it requires specific rules to be adhered to, in order to work effectively. It also requires an active moderator, who is well versed in the techniques required. One approach I have used - with great success - is to actually insist on no talking. I might start with a large fishbone diagram, drawn on a board, or printed on a large sheet on the wall (the bigger, the better!). Once the team have agreed the problem statement (the *what*, *where* and *when* of the problem), we will write that into the head of the fish. Then, I will issue everyone in the team with a set of sticky notes - I will encourage them to write any possible causes on their notes, and stick them onto the diagram, without worrying too much about where they attach them. This can work even better if the group sticks their notes to an empty board, or even a wall.

The desire here is to remove any barriers to thought – or,

rather, to *blinkered* thought. What do I mean by this? Well, in a lot of problem-solving environments, particularly when you have experts on your team, you will find, more often than not, there is a notion that the solution is already known: *"I don't know why we're doing this; it's easy:* X *is caused by* Y*. I've been saying it for years, and no-one ever listens!"* Worse still, if there is a senior manager in the room, the overwhelming temptation is for everyone to fall behind the leader: *"I have seen this before. This is what the cause is, and this is what we are going to do."* When a team follows behind one person, in this type of case, all of the intuition and problem-solving skill of the group is lost; they become shadows, standing behind one idea. However many years of experience that team might have, the only resource drawn upon is the singular experience of the dominant voice. This is where a moderator is required, empowered by techniques such as drawing forth the team suggestions through non-discussion. Of course, reading of others' suggestions is encouraged but, at this stage, it is vital that none of the ideas are challenged; right now, we are happy to go with the mantra that all ideas are good ideas. Whilst, in practice, some of the suggestions will be of less value than others, it may be that these sticky notes, when read by others, reinvigorate the process and spark even better thinking amongst the remainder of the group. Furthermore, when the process begins to run dry, as it inevitably will, you can remind the teams to think about the six headings on the diagram (namely: "Man"; "Machine"; "Measurement"; "Material"; "Method"; and "Environment"), to eke out any remaining thinking. Now we are ready to move onto the next stage.

Taking the notes, we can begin to place them together by theme - or "affinity groups", as some people like to call them. Of course, we can do this just as easily by writing them onto the appropriate arms of the Ishikawa diagram but, in reality, it doesn't matter if the suggestions fall exactly into the right locations or not. It is also possible that some of your notes will equally locate on two or more of the focus categories - again, this doesn't matter: I would rather see the same suggestion on all six arms of my fishbone than it not be there at all!

So, now we have our fishbone diagram filled in; we have completed the head of our fish with the problem statement, and we have collated suggestions as to all of the possible (and improbable) causes to our issue. The main takeaway is that we are thinking. We are now ready to go deeper, and we are ready to prioritize, to allow for even more focused and powerful thinking.

But first, as we have done throughout, let us revisit the topic of the fishbone diagram, only this time with the overlay of our own investigations into personal improvement. By this discussion, we will be approaching the real essence of work, by attempting to identify that which is truly stopping us from being everything that we deserve to be. But, what might such a diagram look like? Below is a potential example:

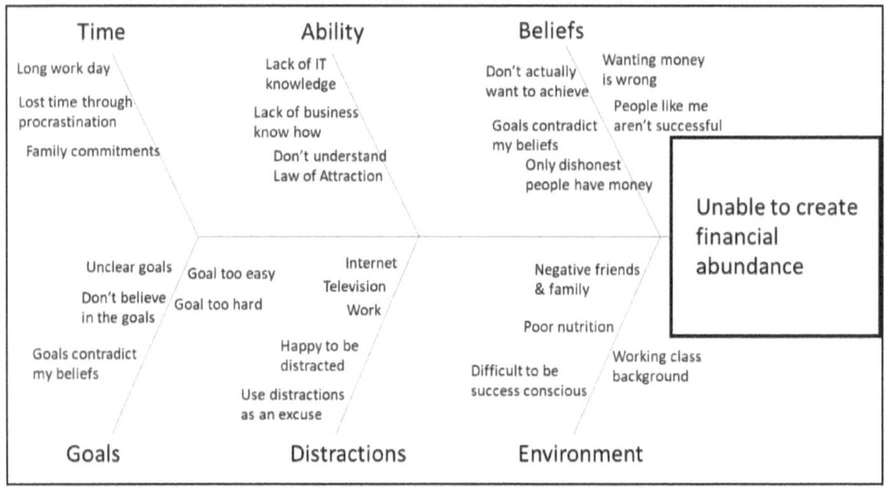

This is one I have put together based on challenges which I have faced in the past, or today. I haven't spent too long on it, but if you are able to spend some time and really – and, I mean *really* - look inside yourself, imagine the sort of insights you could gather! The major difference between this fishbone and the one described above - aside from the category changes - is the lack of a group component. There are two points arising from this.

If you are lucky enough to have a close friend or family member who will call you out and challenge you on these points, then, by all means, go ahead and use them - this would work particularly well if that friend was on a similar path. The value of a mastermind alliance of this nature really cannot be understated. It will also give you the chance to return that service and do the same for your friend - in that way, you will both achieve magnificent value and insight.

However, this is not to denigrate the opportunity which is present in carrying out this activity by yourself. The key, as it always is, is to be unblinkingly honest, and you will only get out what you put in. Besides, what is to be gained from being dishonest with yourself? In theory, this sort of examination sounds easy, but if you find yourself coming up against deeply-held beliefs, it will be anything but. In twelve-step recovery programmes, step four is to "take a searching and fearless moral inventory". When I was first recovering from compulsive gambling - I will be honest - I didn't really face up to this challenge; at the time, my focus was simply on not having a bet. To look deeper into the reasons why I did it in the first place did not seem advisable, particularly given that I would not have been particularly strong at that stage. Fortunately, I had no choice but not to bet: I had no money to bet with, and that money which I did have was being carefully monitored.

It is not what you do when there is no choice which makes the difference: what counts is what you do when choice is restored. Many of us - myself included - have been found wanting at this stage: do you make the tough decision and go after your goals, or do you make the easy choice and dismiss them as mere dreams? If we're taking the tougher route, then it may be that we have to look deeper.

11

ROOT-CAUSE ANALYSIS

In a business environment, my next step would be to isolate and prioritize a few of the suggestions I am interested in looking at further.

In a group environment, this can be done in a number of ways, though voting is as good as any. I like to give each team member three votes on each of the three topics they would like to explore further - it seems to work better than one vote each, as participants cannot merely vote for their own pet idea, and are forced to consider other options. It is what happens next that really counts, however: we carry out further analysis by searching out the root cause.

The method I am going to discuss is a simple yet powerful technique, again of Japanese origin, which can be quite a difficult technique to practice. The technique is called *"5 WHYS"*.

Why? Well, let me attempt to explain. Those of you who have children, grandchildren, nieces, nephews or even younger brothers and sisters will be aware of the arguing prowess of the very young. The winning tactic is relatively simple. Let's try to recreate one such scenario:

Child: "Daddy, can I have an ice-cream?"

Father: "No."

Child: "Why?"

Father: "Because you're going to have your dinner soon."

Child: "Why have I got to have dinner?"

Father: "Because, if you don't, you won't grow big and strong."

Child: "Why?"

Father: "Because what you eat helps you grow."

Child: "But, I can eat an ice-cream. Why can't I have an ice-cream?"

Father: "Because I said so!"

Skewed logic, perhaps, but this is what we need to do with our problem: we need to back it into a corner, until it has no choice but to give us the only answer.

Let me illustrate further. I used to have a car - it was quite an old car, but I liked it, and it gave me good service. The only problem was that it seemed to go through headlamp bulbs like a Christmas tree! I was doing a fair few miles back then and did a lot of driving in the dark, so it was particularly evident when a bulb had gone, especially on the unlit country roads. Luckily, there was a shop near me which provided a replacement bulb service and was open until eight o'clock at night. I would often find myself swinging by, just before it closed, to purchase a bulb and have it fitted. Then, the following morning, I would be merrily on my way, fully illuminated for both myself and my fellow road users... at least, for another few days, when the other one would go out! And so, I would continue on this cycle: left lamp out; replace bulb; right lamp out; replace bulb; left lamp out; replace bulb, etc., etc., etc., ad infinitum...

So, what was I doing – or, rather, what was I not doing? Exactly: I was never diagnosing the root cause of my problem! I was merely addressing the symptom: bulb out – replace bulb. So, why was I surprised when this issue kept returning? In business, we do this all the time: we put a temporary fix in place, just to keep the production line running. Unfortunately, the daily targets take over and that temporary fix becomes the permanent solution. We end up firefighting, crisis management, call it what you will; we create teams of roving troubleshooters, who just go around putting out the same old fires, with the same old temporary fixes, and we greet them as heroes - all because we've never stopped to solve the problem, once and for all, at its root cause, when it first occurs.

Remember Hansei, the concept of stepping back and becoming a learning organization? If we think back to my car, the correct response would have been to put it into the garage for diagnostic work, to check for electrical faults - there was obviously some bigger fault at play.

So, why didn't I? Well, again the answer is simple: I needed the car to get me to work, the following morning - this was my justification for the temporary fix. I was also trying to dodge the initial capital outlay. But, how many bulbs would I replace before that initial outlay stopped becoming an effective cost avoidance? I was stuck in the short-termism which afflicts us all, at every level of society: unless we are willing to plan for the long-term, we will continue to make decisions which might not resonate with our long-term wellbeing. At the risk of disappearing on a tangent, our method of government struggles with this issue: with only five years in office, you cannot really plan for ten or twenty years ahead; at most, you can probably look four years into the future and, even then, only in the knowledge that you have to make the more popular decisions to ensure re-election; it becomes tough to have the really difficult discussions.

But, back to us. We have clearly seen the need to address

the blocks to our potential, at a root-cause level; it is sometimes not enough to use sheer willpower and habit. We have already hinted at one technique to drive toward the identification of those deeply hidden root causes. This is *"5 WHY Root Cause Analysis"*.

The method, as we have seen, seems simple, but this can be a deceptively difficult piece of work. Below you will find an example of a 5 WHY Root Cause Analysis table. Here, *"why?"* has actually been asked six times, from the first suggestion, which I explored in my Ishikawa diagram, in order to illustrate that it doesn't actually have to be five *whys* - sometimes it will be two; sometimes it will be twenty. Sometimes, the thinking may branch off and present multiple root causes.

Unable to create financial abundance	
Why am I unable to create financial abundance?	*Because I lose time through procrastination...*
Why do I lose time through procrastination?	*Because I find it difficult to get going...*
Why do I find it difficult to get going?	*Because I don't want to progress the project...*
Why don't I want to progress the project?	*Because I don't want to finish it...*
Why don't I want to finish it?	*Because I don't want to have it judged...*
Why don't I want to have it judged?	*Because I don't want to know that it is not good enough...*
Why don't I want to know if the project is not good enough?	*Because I am afraid of failing.*
Root cause: I have a fear of failure.	

I guess the key here is not to go in with any expectations. It is so easy to have an answer wedged in your mind and steer your thinking toward it. This is what makes this technique so difficult and, at the same time, so very rewarding. If you can really let yourself go and surrender to this technique, there is no telling what you might be gifted.

So, the point of the Ishikawa diagram and 5 WHY Root Cause Analysis becomes clear: it is those issues identified at a root cause which we need to work on.

Let's say that I am focusing on my desire to be a writer. I could, using the detail in the diagram above, focus my efforts on overcoming procrastination. Maybe that could be through designing reward systems such as those we have described before: e.g. allowing myself to watch my favourite programme after I have typed a prerequisite number of words. But, in reality, I am going to struggle. I might meet my goal for several days, but even on the occasions that I do meet this target, I am still finding it difficult to settle into work. The truth of the matter is that, throughout this whole time, it is not my inability to quickly settle into writing which is the problem: what I am actually trying to combat is a deep-rooted, fear-based emotion - in this case, my fear of failure.

If it turns out that I am actually not going to achieve my desire - something which I have defined as my life purpose - then where does that leave me? Perhaps it is better that I only try half-heartedly, and leave that element of doubt on the table - that *what could have been,* so that I can hide in that area of ambiguity created by my procrastination: *"I could have been a great writer if I didn't need to work full-time"; "I could have been a millionaire if I'd had the right education"; "I could live a fulfilled life if I had been born into better circumstances"...* The ambiguity is where the ready-made excuses live - the task now is to push through that. Surely, it is better to have lived knowing that you really tried, rather than to live with the ghosts of lives which never, ever were.

In this day and age, when everything is so quick, it is tempting to want instant solutions to our problems - this is where our love of quick fixes come from. I must admit, I find it very difficult to understand people who "fall out" with others. What does this really mean? Does it actually mean that we lack the desire to push through our fears and understand what truly lies at the bottom of the issue? The same is true of our calling in life; so many of us give up at the first temporary defeat. We then spend a lot of time and effort creating excuses, which we repeat so often that we actually end up believing them ourselves.

That last sentence is so important that it is worth revisiting and rewording; I had not planned to think about it here, but the flow of my writing has brought me to it.

What we repeat to ourselves, backed by emotion, is actually taken over by the subconscious and communicated to the Universe! This idea repeats, over and over again in the classic *Think and Grow Rich*, by Napoleon Hill. Similar ideas are built upon, when the power of prayer is discussed in the book *The Isaiah Effect*, by Gregg Braden. Our mind is truly awesome and powerful - surely it is worth the effort to diagnose the root causes of what might be stopping it from running smoothly?

Business suffers from this sort of angst, as well. We spoke earlier about the damaging effects of short-termism in business; employees want to make their mark and they want to make it now. This is why it is so easy to go after short-term targets, particularly when management seems to be on a two-year merry-go-round of role swapping. Nobody wants to be sat in an interview or a review, with a handful of long-term objectives which have barely begun; people want the snap, snap, snap of achievements, regardless of the less appealing long-term impact of the decision making. This means that real root-cause work - particularly that on an organizational level - never gets done; there is no appetite. The quick sprint wins over the long, hard slog every time, particularly when the timescale for return on investment begins to stretch.

I guess the irony lies in the fact that companies don't actually exist - not really. This might sound strange, but let's give it some thought. What is a business? It is a collection of people, working together, to create something of value for another set of people. Everybody would describe themselves as working for "the business", but the truth is that this is a very abstract thing. Maybe that is one of the reasons why we invest in corporate buildings, identifiable logos and recognizable uniforms: it all drives the illusion. True, the sum of the parts will be greater, but if a business is a functioning collection of people, why would we expect it to behave any differently from, and have different problems to, those which we experience as a single individual? We *all* need to work on the true root causes of what is holding us back.

12

VISION STATEMENTS, MISSION STATEMENTS, CORE VALUES, CUSTOMER ORIENTATION, ALIGNMENT AND PRIORITIZATION

The header for this section may seem confused and convoluted. It may also appear to be something of a leap from where we have just been working. But, I think there is value to be drawn here. Let's begin with some definitions.

A "Vision Statement" is a written declaration of the desired future position of a business. It is a description of how the business will look at a defined point in the future, given a successful future state. It is not too much of a leap to realize that we ourselves, as developing and growing individuals, should have a Vision Statement, too. Makes sense, doesn't it?

So, here is a task which you can do, here and now: write your Vision Statement. Write about how you have met the purpose in your life and what your life now looks like. Let the shackles fall free! Write in detail about all of the positivity and abundance present in all areas of your life. Maybe you would also like to see this in images. This is where you could also create a vision board, with pictures of that perfect home, that dream car, that idyllic holiday destination - whatever it is that you see in that amazing future, to which you are perfectly entitled, and which is inevitably and certainly coming to you! Your Vision Statement defines your long-term future success, so go big and get excited!

The "Mission Statement" is a little closer to home: it describes what you are prepared to do today and over the next year, say. So, what are you going to do today, tomorrow, next week, next month, and how does this further your business – or, in our case, yourself, in pursuit of your vision? Your Mission Statement will undoubtedly change, year on year, but you should still be able to discern your core values within it: e.g. those principles of being, which are important to you. In this sense, our values, our mission and our vision are all aligned, and nothing is in a contrary position. Think back to our Ishikawa diagram: am I going to find it easy to create financial abundance, when the whole time one of my secret values is that the pursuit of money is in some way negative?

It is worth doing significant work in all three of these areas: what is important to you in life; why is it important; are you living in alignment with those values which you hold to be significant to your direction in life?

What does your future vision look like? What do you do? Where do you live? How do you show gratitude for the things you have? What are your relationships like, and how do they add growth, healing and positivity to your life? How does your abundance make you feel? See it; touch it; taste it... back it with a sense of satisfaction and gratitude. Call it into your mind on a daily basis, at least, and live like it has already happened!

Finally, what are you going to do today to take a step closer to that goal? What are you going to do tomorrow, next week and next month? How are you going to hold yourself accountable for achieving these goals? Could you find an online support group of likeminded individuals?

In terms of customer orientation, all businesses should be focused entirely on the customer; it is the customer who defines everything. They define quality, cost, demand and what denotes satisfaction. In the final analysis, the customer pays the bills and therefore defines what is of value. If your customer could see everything that goes on in your business – and, by that, I mean *absolutely* everything - do you think that they would be willing to pay for it? Most definitely not, but the truth is that they are already paying for it; every time an organization creates one of the eight wastes, the customer foots the bill. By removing the waste from our processes, we increase the value that the customer receives. This gives us interesting choices: we can reduce the price of our product or, better still, hold it, while our rivals are being forced to raise theirs. Furthermore, we can do this while increasing our profit margin, by creating even more value-adding processes, with the resources we already have. In short, we can bring in more orders, or create more products, without increasing our headcount. So, naturally, the whole organization should be aligned to the needs of the customer and, through them, the needs of the dedicated grassroots staff, who are nearest to the customer and reside at the point of value creation.

This discussion can be widened, too. Whilst we are

primarily thinking about our external customers - those good people who are actually buying the product - this logic, of course, extends to our internal customers, too. Our internal customer can be defined as the next person in the process - the value-added function, to which we supply work. This person or team have exactly the same needs as our external customer: they require the product to reach them to the correct quality, in the correct quantity and at the right time - even better if this replenishment can take place exactly as the previous work or parts are consumed. That way, we can set up true lean, *just-in-time* supply, with the ideal batch size of single-piece flow.

So, it stands to reason that in order to align ourselves to our customer desires and expectations, we first need to understand what those desires and expectations are. However, you would be surprised how many companies overlook this simple fact and push their ideas onto the customer, often in the guise of innovations. There is a logic to this, but only if the customers have been consulted, perhaps through questionnaires, focus groups or other types of market research - guessing is simply not good enough. The temptation to keep innovating, however, is well-founded, as we have said. Take a look at the diagram below:

This simple chart is called a "Kano Diagram". As you can see, the *dissatisfaction* region on this model is defined as anything below the "Expected Quality" line, and "Basic Quality" sits wholly within the dissatisfied area! What is clear, though, is that the *satisfaction* region exists exclusively in the area above the "Exciting Quality" curve. The mobile phone industry is a clear example of this type of thinking. If we think back to what our mobile phones looked like fifteen or twenty years ago, the difference is startling. The device would have been huge, and it would have been able to make calls (once you pulled out the aerial!), perhaps send texts and have one or two rudimentary games - this, in those days, was actually Exciting Quality. Now, even Expected Quality is tremendously advanced from these early pioneer models. We expect our phones to have cameras able to take pictures with clarity which could only be dreamt of by the professional photographers of yesteryear. We want to be able to connect to the internet; do our banking; buy groceries; or, arrange tickets to some sought-after event. We want to be able to connect with our families and friends, over a variety of platforms. We want our phones to do everything which, just a few short years ago, only our computers could handle. In short, our virtual lives have become something of our extended reality. The definition of "Exciting Quality" in this sector is redefined with a speed which is mind-blowing. Indeed, it seems that our imagination is the only barrier to what this technology might eventually be able to do.

This has placed innovators in the high-end world of electronic technology in an envied position: this elite, empowered by the knowledge to make our dreams come true, are actually in a position to now tell us what our dreams are, and market them directly to us. We can see this with our own eyes, when we witness the enthusiasm created by the release of a new wonder-phone or games console. Any firms without the research budget, and those which could not market "Exciting Quality", have gone the way of the dinosaurs.

You can be the customer of your own life! You can define what Exciting Quality is, and actively pursue it. Most of us live our lives in the Basic Quality region of the Kano Diagram and, at the very best, touch the Expected Quality line occasionally. For most, this is fine, and there is nothing wrong with it. These people work all year, and perhaps have ten days in the sun, once a year; they are relatively happy in their work and in their relationships, and they can afford a few nice things for their homes. But, even these people sometimes wonder what an "exciting quality" of life might feel like. We all do; this is the human condition. You are reading this because you want to improve your life; you are part of this journey.

We are all connected, and we all have an inkling that there is something else. It is startling just how many belief systems describe a loss - a separation from a forgotten well of human knowledge. But, I sense there are those which are now waking. Maybe it is the next step in human evolution. We live in our own organic internet, linked by the electrical matrix of the Earth. Gregg Braden reminds us of the Hopi Indians, whose ancient mythology describes a great spider web, which encompasses us all.

I am digressing a little, but I think the point is an

important one: in these days of the lurking threat of war and economic and environmental delicacy, I am filled with tremendous hope. There are enough of us who are waking, and the internet links us together. If we can all align what Exciting Quality looks like for our future, there is no telling what we can do. Look at what a few experts have done with the mobile phone! Thirty or forty years ago, there were those innovators who dared to dream. Technology has advanced during our lifetimes quicker than it did across the hundreds of years which preceded them. There is nothing that a waking humanity cannot achieve, including world peace, prosperity and stability. You are a part of that journey.

So, to come back to our original point, be the customer of your life; define what Exciting Quality means to you. Furthermore, define it without reference to what you feel is possible.

I say this with some confidence, because I strongly suspect that when you really look at what you want, sure, you will identify financial abundance, but you will also find that you want to do good works with that abundance - to share it with friends, family and those less fortunate. You will be struck with a burning desire to share what you have learnt; to induce others to join you; to take up the light and shine it into the world. This is the momentum that I sense has started. This is the hope for all of our collective futures, as the positivity and love permeating the Hopi web links us all.

By this time, you will, no doubt, have a collection of actions and suggestions which you have collated during the *PLAN* phase of your PDCA Cycle. But, this can be a tricky time. It is possible that you have identified quite a number of actions, and you are now overwhelmed. What should you start with?

There are a number of tools which you can use to help you, should you be unable to see the natural narrative, or critical pathway, of your journey. The simplest of these tools is the "Prioritization Matrix". Here is an example:

Prioritization Matrix For Starting an Online Business:

Benefit \ Effort	Low	Medium	High
High	Come up with a catchy name	Research similar sites already out there / Research products	Define & deploy my marketing strategy
Medium		Research hosting options	
Low	Sketch ideas for logos		Learn code

Effort

As you can see, the Prioritization Matrix is a straightforward graphical representation of an action, the benefit that action derives, and how much effort is required to deliver that action.

In Kaizen, this graph can be useful, because it points us toward the quick wins and potentially stops us from carrying out work which is going to give us little in return. This is a great tool for identifying which actions to do first, particularly in an improvement project (or problem-solving) environment. One criticism is that a matrix of this type encourages project teams to go after the low-hanging fruit first: e.g. the easier actions to address. But, don't forget that these actions have also been deemed to have the biggest impact.

If we are using this tool to weigh up the relative merits of problem-solving activities, the tasks placed in the Prioritization Matrix will be direct countermeasures to the root causes we previously identified, using our Ishikawa diagram and 5 WHY Root Cause Analysis. Here, the advantage of getting big wins on the board quickly cannot be underestimated: these wins will create momentum, and will also make management sit up and support the more difficult tasks to come.

We have essentially been speaking about momentum throughout; the need to start with a tangible result cannot be underestimated. In such a problem-solving-orientated Prioritization Matrix, it may be that we don't actually complete all of the tasks described; we may find that those tasks in the bottom right-hand corner are prohibitive. Cost-benefit analysis may show that the expense of completing a particular piece of work far outweighs the return that work offers. In this case, there is a clear business decision to be made.

However, the work that you and I are doing - as individuals interested in personal improvement and self-realization - may not lend itself ideally to such a tool. In the example given above, all of the tasks will need to be completed, to achieve the planned outcome: in our example, the successful launch of a small online business. Rather, we need a different tool to highlight the relationship between the tasks and to place them in a structured, chronological order. The Gantt Chart is one such tool:

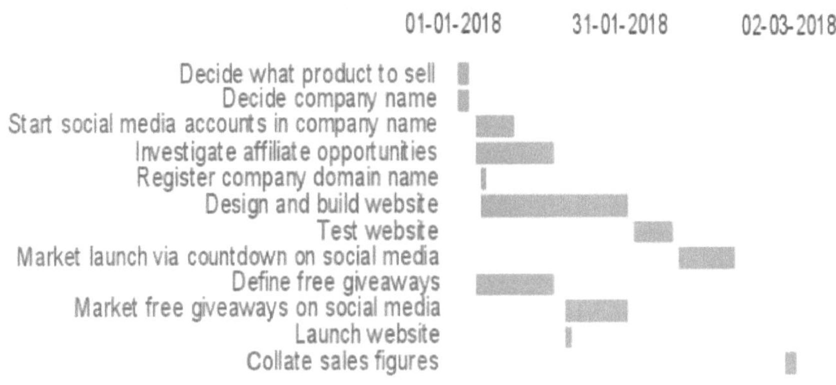

Again, I have used the simple example of setting up an online business, though I would not necessarily follow these steps if you are planning to set something up - the purpose of this chart is to display the power of the tool, rather than the accuracy of the steps. What we can see here is the way that the tasks relate to one another: e.g. their dependencies. There will be some tasks which can or must start at the same time, some that have to finish before the next task can begin (i.e. you cannot test the website until you have built it) and those work packages which have to finish at the same time;

these will typically be jobs which can be done simultaneously, but have a defined, shared endpoint. What is clear is that most of the work needs to be done prior to the launch of our website - afterwards, the real work of the continuous marketing and product innovation begins.

I am going to talk about one last tool in this section, but it is not one which I will cover in much depth. It is called "Quality Function Deployment" (QFD). QFD can be a tremendously complex tool, used for aligning the work that a business does with the things which are important to its customer. It is used to focus the resources of the business to these areas of customer importance, in a structured and mathematical way. I have enjoyed some success in the past, using a much-simplified element of this tool, and it is this singular element which I am going to present to you now. However, if you are intrigued by this tool, you will find plenty of useful resources online.

House of Quality for my Online Business	Weighting	% Repeat Business	% Visits leading to sale	No. of visitors (month)	No. of affiliates	Clicks to purchase	% Upsells	Mean time between updates	Quality of feedback	Totals
Weighting		2.0	1.8	1.9	1.0	1.2	1.6	1.0	2.0	
Good product range	1.5	9	9	3	3	1	9	1	9	66
Quality materials	2.0	9	3	3	3	1	3	1	9	64
Easy to navigate	1.2	3	9	9	3	9	3	3	9	58
Reliable shopping and payment	1.7	9	9	1	1	3	9	1	9	71
Excellent customer support	1.0	9	9	3	3	1	3	1	9	38
Totals		78	70	36	13	18	43	7	90	
		95%	10%	10k	20	<5	50%	1	90%	

Strong correlation	9
Medium correlation	3
Weak correlation	1

So, let us break this down a little. The column on the left lists the things which would be important to the customers of our fictional online business. The next column is what we feel would be the relative weight assigned by the customer. I have used a relatively condensed scale of 0.0 (not important at all) to 2.0 (very important) - wider scales can be used but, on my system here, the impact would be great. The rows, as you can see, will be the metrics by which we would measure the success of the critical customer requirements. For example, one metric of how well our product range is being received would be a measure of what percentage of our customers return for repeat purchases. The numbers in the central panel are our thoughts on the correlation between the two considerations on the intersection. For example: our research may have shown that there is a strong correlation between "Repeat business" and "Good product range"; alternatively, there is only a weak correlation between having a reliable payment system and the number of visitors (i.e. people will only discover the reliability of our payment system once something has already brought them to the site). You will notice that I have filled in all of the correlation value boxes, though in most examples you will usually see that boxes are left blank where there is no correlation, as opposed to a weak one: I find it just as easy to fill in all of the values, particularly as the lower value of one has minimal impact, when compared with the upper value of nine. The final scores, in each direction, are calculated as the sum of the correlation values, multiplied by the weight of the appropriate customer need (the *what*) or the key metric (the *how*).

The results can sometimes be surprising. In terms of the above example, a reliable shopping and payment experience ranks as the top customer expectation from our site; it would appear that difficulty in checking out their shopping cart is more important than our producing a wide range of quality materials! Whilst there is a lot to be said for a good range of quality products – the only reason why customers return to make repeat purchases – in the rush to get these items to market, it is possible that we may be less focused on the shopping experience. It is no use having great products if your customers abandon the notion of buying them midway through the transaction, so this particular *"House of Quality"* reminds us to place appropriate effort into the functionality of our website, ensuring that it is easy to use and that our potential prospects are converted into returning buyers, who then provide us with marketing, through social media.

True, we may not have overlooked this anyway, but the driver behind this section on Vision Statements, Mission Statements, core values, customer orientation, alignment and prioritization has been to provide us with sharp focus and clarity about where we need to do our work, and how we cut through the confusion of competing priorities.

13

HANSEI

And, so we come back to the concept of Hansei. If you remember, Hansei is the central idea of stepping back and reflecting where you are. We can also combine it with the concept of *"Yokoten"*, which roughly means "across everywhere".

When I first started learning about Kaizen, the eight wastes and Continuous Improvement, it was as if a curtain had been drawn back. A lot of Continuous Improvement professionals describe this feeling; it is something of the "curse" of the trade: once seen, it can never be unseen. You may also find this, having read this book. When you go to the shops, or a restaurant, you will begin to see examples of the wastes we have described: maybe you will see a waiter or a waitress taking a convoluted route, or making a journey whilst unladen; maybe you will see a huge pile of pre-made boxes, taking up space and waiting for pizzas; perhaps you will see a supermarket worker walking to and from a storage cage, to place tins onto an empty shelf. Whatever it is -

however these wastes manifest themselves - you will see them, and it will take all of your self-control not to intervene and work with the person to find a better way. If you do jump in, make your intervention sustainable and use the *GROW* coaching model to derive benefit for your coachee!

But, it is your self-reflection, moving forward, which will be absolutely key, for it is you that you are trying to reconcile yourself with. This book has been about finding practical tools with which you can identify those limiting beliefs and norms which are holding you back, and start to work on them in a structured way. When we spoke about Vision Statements, we were really talking about the vision that you have for your own life, and how you might define a prioritized action plan to get there. For certain, this is going to entail working on yourself; convincing yourself that you are worthy - that you are entitled to bring this vision to fruition, and that you are able to be anything that you want to be.

Don't apologize for that! In fact, be thankful for it! Give thanks for the life that you want to lead, before it has arrived. The Universe will not know the difference, and your frequency will naturally rise to the required level - the trick is to keep it there. This infers everything that we have been talking about, during this book. We need continuous, consistent, focused action, toward a defined target point, with our milestones pencilled in along the way. We need the momentum of our early victories - perhaps delivered through *5S* - and we need the constant affirmation of our purpose, which we will bring to our mind as often as we possibly can, simultaneously feeling the joy and the gratitude that our inevitable and already present success brings us.

Along the way, we celebrate and give thanks for what we currently have. We give service and share our abundance with others. We seek out and associate with people who have trod or are on the path we wish to tread. We appropriate their knowledge, and we give thanks by supporting and cheering on others. We commit to improving our lives, in one small way, every single day that we are blessed with existence. We daily, consistently and continuously Kaizen our lives.

ABOUT THE AUTHOR

Simon D. Gary has been on a Continuous Improvement journey for the last ten years. He has trained lean manufacturing techniques in many different industry sectors, including healthcare, electronics, papermaking, aerospace, hospitality and the food industry.

Simon is currently working with one of the most prestigious global names in the automotive industry, applying daily the same techniques you have read about in this book.

Simon has also used this knowledge to beat a gambling problem, write a successful novel and set-up two high-performing websites and blogs.

You can replicate, exceed and enjoy your successes with the insights provided by *Kaizen Your Life*. Join Simon at *www.simondgary.com* and tell him all about it!

GLOSSARY

5 WHYS: The practice of asking "why?" of circumstance 5 times, in order to uncover the root-cause reason for a problem. The root cause is found when the question "why?" can no longer be answered. If the true root cause is addressed, the problem should not recur.

5S: A five-step process, designed to align a work environment to support the work that is done. *5S* is also the primary tool used to eliminate waste within the system., as well as the foundation for all lean improvement. The five stages of *5S* are: *SORT, SET, SHINE, STANDARDIZE* and *SUSTAIN.*

8 WASTES: The eight wastes present in any process, namely: transportation; inventory; motion; waiting; overproduction; overprocessing; defects; and, skills and suggestions. This list is equally applicable to manufacturing and transactional environments.

AUTONOMOUS MAINTENANCE (AM): The small, daily maintenance tasks carried out on a machine by its operator. This might include checking lubricants and levels. See also TPM.

CAUSE AND EFFECT DIAGRAM: A diagram which draws together all of the possible causes for a problem, to allow for further analysis. This would normally be the forerunner of *5 WHY ROOT CAUSE ANALYSIS*. The diagram is usually presented with six arms: man, method, machine, material, measurement and environment – although, these can be changed, dependent on need.

CYCLE TIME: The amount of time taken to complete one cycle of a process, from start to finish. It should ideally be around 90% of the *TAKT* time. Cycle time will include many of the eight wastes, so can be decreased through waste elimination.

DEFECT: A defect is defined as any deviation from the standard. Defects cause two additional cost streams: scrap and rework. The farther away from the source of creation that a defect is found, the greater the cost to the business.

FIFO: *"First in, first out"* - a system which ensures the oldest material or product is consumed first. A supermarket must ensure that they adhere to this concept.

FISH: *"First in, still here"* - the opposite of *FIFO*.

FISHBONE DIAGRAM: See *CAUSE AND EFFECT DIAGRAM.*

GANTT CHART: A project management tool which defines the timeline and critical path through a set of project actions. It will highlight certain relationships between actions: e.g. those actions which must start together; those which must finish before others can start; and, those which must finish together.

GEMBA: Literally the place where the work is done; the office or shop floor. Interestingly, it also means "crime scene" in Japanese - as in, the best chance to solve a crime is when you see it happen!

GROW: A coaching model, based on steering a coachee through the steps of: *GOAL, REALITY, OBSTACLES* and *WILL.* This ideally occurs in a topic in which the coachee is not comfortable, meaning the coachee is in their personal learning zone and genuinely grows from the experience. Application of a coaching model is one of the hallmarks of an organizational learning culture.

HANSEI: The concept of stepping back and reflecting - the hallmark of a learning organization.

ISHIKAWA DIAGRAM: See *CAUSE AND EFFECT DIAGRAM.*

JIT: *"Just in time"* - a delivery or replenishment system which plans for material or product to be made available, just as it is required. *JIT* is one of the indicators of a "pull system", and reduces the wastes of inventory and waiting (see also *8 WASTES*).

KAIZEN: A Japanese term, literally meaning "change for the good" or "change for the better". It has come to be synonymous with the concept of Continuous Improvement. *KAIZEN* is the responsibility of everybody within the enterprise, and is most effectively achieved by those who do the actual work under scrutiny.

KANBAN: A signal to "pull" material through a system; a flag or card, which indicates that material needs to be replenished (see also *JIT*).

KANO DIAGRAM: A theoretical diagram which shows the link between quality, innovation and customer satisfaction.

KATA: In martial arts, *KATA* are the set moves practiced by a practitioner to achieve mastery and muscle memory. In the workplace, *KATA* refers to a structured set of questions which guide a team member through an improvement or coaching cycle (see also *GROW*).

KPI: *"Key Performance Indicator"* - a measure which provides a snapshot of how well we are doing at this moment in time. KPIs should be up to date, easy to interpret and displayed in a relevant location. Those reading the KPI should know how they can influence it.

LAW OF ATTRACTION: The law which states that whatever you constantly bring into your mind, via thought and gratitude, will be magnetically drawn toward you. Popularized in many classic books, such as *Think and Grow Rich*, by Napoleon Hill, and *The Secret*, by Rhonda Byrne

LCL: *"Lower Control Limit"* - the smallest end of a specification: e.g. the minimum width permissible; anything below this specification is a defect.

LEARNING ORGANIZATION: An organization committed to continually improving by learning from their mistakes and growing every individual in the enterprise. Creating a learning organization is one of the foundations of the successful lean enterprise.

MASTERMIND ALLIANCE: A group of like-minded people, who support one another in the pursuit of their goals.

MEAN TIME TO FAILURE (MTTF): The mean time

between the failures of an unrepairable system.

MEAN TIME TO REPAIR (MTTR): The mean time between repairs to a repairable system.

MISSION STATEMENT: A short-term statement of intent, linking the current condition to the longer-term vision.

MUDA: The Japanese term for the eight wastes. One of the three Ms.

MURA: *"Unevenness"* - a wasteful aspect of work. One of the three Ms.

MURI: *"Overburden"* - a wasteful aspect of work. One of the three Ms.

NON-VALUE-ADDED WORK: Activity which is necessary, under the current circumstances, but does not change the function, fit or form of the product. An example might be performing a test or scanning a part; inspection is typically a non-value-added process.

OEE: *"Overall Equipment Effectiveness"*. OEE is a rolled measure of the *availability x performance x quality* of a piece of equipment or machine. See also *AUTONOMOUS MAINTENANCE, PLANNED MAINTENANCE* and *TPM*.

PDCA CYCLE: *"PLAN; DO; CHECK; ACT."* - a four-stage improvement cycle. It is typified by the following steps:
PLAN: Make a plan for an improvement;
DO: trial the improvement;
CHECK: check that the improvement was successful;
ACT: If it was, train out and standardize the improvement.

If the improvement failed, ask "What have we learnt?" and return to the *PLAN* phase.

PLANNED MAINTENANCE: Large scale maintenance of machines, carried out during a pre-planned period: e.g. the servicing of a car.

POKA YOKE: *"Mistake-proofing".* A three-pin plug is a perfect *POKA-YOKE* device, as it can only be fitted into the socket in one orientation.

PRIORITIZATION MATRIX: A tool which references the viability of an action by comparing the amount of effort required and the value of the outcome. Low effort, high benefit actions are usually completed first.

PULL: A system which only replenishes what has been consumed. The customer receives only what they need, exactly when they need it.

PUSH: A system which moves product on when it is finished, regardless of whether it is needed by the customer. The presence of a push system will be noticeable by piles of inventory between processes.

QCD: *"Quality, cost and delivery"* - the magic triangle of any process. *Right-first-time* quality will reduce costs, increase delivery schedule achievement and, ultimately, increase profit margins.

QFD: *"Quality Function Deployment"* - a matrix which quantifies the link between a process or action and its importance to the customer. It ensures that focus is placed on those features most important to the customer.

RISK ASSESSMENT: An activity which identifies the risk in a process - often completed by quantifying and multiplying the severity and likelihood of an outcome, and considering what control measures are also in place. It can then be determined if these measures are enough, or more needs to be done to protect against the risk.

ROOT CAUSE: The real cause of a problem. If this is addressed properly, the problem should not recur; where the problem returns, the initial solution has only been addressed at a symptomatic level

ROOT CAUSE ANALYSIS: See *5 WHYS.*

SET-UP REDUCTION: The activity concerned with reducing the time taken for a machine set-up, between producing the last good part of product A and producing the first good part of product B.

SINGLE MINUTE EXCHANGE OF DIES: See *SET-UP REDUCTION.*

SKILLS MATRIX: A document which details the level of competency of team members, in various tasks. It usually displays five levels of competence: no skill; under training with constant supervision; under training with periodic supervision; fully competent; can train others.

SPC: *"Statistical Process Control"* - a scientific method of measuring if a process output remains around the nominal value, and does not track toward, or exceed, the *LCL* or *UCL*: e.g. the part being produced remains within the acceptable engineering tolerances.

STANDARD OPERATING PROCEDURE: The document

which states what needs to happen, to turn an input into an output. It may also state how this is to be done, and incorporate care points, safety points and know-how from the operator team.

STANDARDIZATION: The activity of ensuring that processes can be followed consistently, to produce repeatable and reproducible outcomes.
STANDARDIZATION is the single best method that we know of today; without it, we do not have a stable baseline upon which to build the next improvement. In turn, the updated standard ensures that the improvement is embedded. Standards are organic and are best improved by those who do the work; they are one of the prerequisites of the learning organization and are a cornerstone of lean methods

TAKT: The amount of production time available, divided by the customer demand; the "heartbeat" of a process. A TAKTed system will prevent overproduction and will deliver product *JIT.*

TIMWOODS: See *8 WASTES.*

TPM: *"Total Productive Maintenance"* - a business-wide approach to reducing waste and maximizing output. *5S, AUTONOMOUS MAINTENANCE* and *PLANNED MAINTENANCE* are all pillars of this system.

TPS: The *"Toyota Production System"* - the lighthouse of global lean. Much envied and much copied, the overarching principles of *TPS* are respect for people and the creation of a learning environment.

UCL: *"Upper Control Limit"* - the maximum permissible value of a variable: e.g. the longest a piece can be, before it is considered a defect.

VALUE-ADDED WORK: Any work which changes the fit, form or function of a product or output, in line with customer requirements: e.g. fitting a part or preparing a document. Another way of thinking about it is "the work for which the customer is willing to pay."

VALUE-STREAM MAP: A diagrammatic representation of how material and information flows through your system, for a particular product family. The map is very useful for spotting blocks and opportunities to improve. A product family might have multiple maps: e.g. *"Current State"*, *"Intermediate Future States"* and *"Ideal State".*

VISION STATEMENT: The communication of the desired future target condition of a business or department. This would typically be reached by achieving multiple intermediate states.

VISUAL MANAGEMENT: The creation of a working system which operates by clear visual cues. The visual workplace will also indicate where opportunities to improve exist, and provide maximum transparency. What we cannot see, we cannot fix.

WORKPLACE ORGANIZATION (5S): See *5S.*